Superfood Smoothies

Superfoods with Smoothies for Weightloss

Deborah Lopez and Tammy Walker

Copyright © 2013 Deborah Lopez and Tammy Walker
All rights reserved.

Table of Contents

INTRODUCTION 1

SECTION 1: SMOOTHIE DIET COOKBOOK 6
    The Benefits of a Smoothie Diet, Fruits in Particular 7
    The Benefits of Drinking Green Smoothies 12
    Lose Weight and Fat on the Smoothie Diet 15
    Smoothie Creations - A Quick How To Guide 15
    Tips for Making Good Smoothies 18

FRUIT SMOOTHIES 21
    Peanut Banana Berry Smoothie 21
    Blackberry Banana Smoothie 23
    Spicy Banana Smoothie 24
    Watermelon Banana Berry Smoothie 25
    Mango Papaya Smoothie 26
    Banana Coconut Smoothie 27
    Fruit Spread Smoothie 28
    Nothing But Fruit Smoothie 29
    Creamy Strawberry Smoothie 30
    Apple Spice Smoothie 31
    Banana Berry Vanilla Smoothie 32
    Refreshing Smoothie 33
    Peachy Banana Berry Vanilla Smoothie 34
    Extra Large Fruit Punch Smoothie 35
    Raspberry Banana Smoothie 36
    Mango Banana Smoothie 37
    Vanilla Orange Banana Smoothie 38
    Purple Smoothie 39
    Fruit Milky Smoothie 40
    Strawberry Pear Smoothie 41
    Spicy Banana Smoothie 42
    PB Banana Smoothie 43
    Herbed Strawberry Mango Smoothie 44
    Orange Berry All Fruit Smoothie 45
    Berry Berry Smoothie 46

Blueberry Banana Protein Smoothie 47
Mango Blueberry Smoothie 48
Tapioca Chai Smoothie 49
Refreshingly Fruity Smoothie 51
Cherry Lemon Banana Smoothie 52
Berry Good Cherry Smoothie 53
Hot Chocolate Strawberry Smoothie 54
Hot Chocolate Blueberry Smoothie 55
Banana Cherry Cordial Smoothie 56
Simple Chocolate Peanut Butter Banana Smoothie 57
Acai Cinnamon Berry Smoothie 58
Spicy Pear Smoothie 59
Sweet Banana Nut Smoothie 60
Hot Chocolate Dessert Smoothie 61
Orange Berry Banana Smoothie 62
Fig Smoothie 63
Minty Melon-Umber Smoothie 64
Tangerine Smoothie 65
Sweet Mango Smoothie 66
Almond Banana Smoothie 67
Pumpkin Smoothie 68
Oatmeal and Fruit Smoothie 69
Pomegranate Smoothie 70
Melon Smoothie 71

VEGETABLE SMOOTHIES (ALSO KNOWN AS GREEN SMOOTHIES) 72

Veggie Nut Smoothie 72
Creamy Papaya Smoothie 74
Strawberry Mud Smoothie 75
Zucchini Orange Smoothie 76
Silly Sweet Zucchini Smoothie 77
California Delight Smoothie 78
Pineapple Kiwi Smoothie 79
Melon Cucumber Broccoli Smoothie 80
Truly Green Smoothie 81
CocoCranNut Smoothie 82
Gingered Veggie Fruit Smoothie 84
Rhubarb Fruit Smoothie 86
Banana Chocolate Mint Green Smoothie 87

Spicy Tomato Smoothie 89
Broccoli Smoothie 90
Orange Carrot Cantaloupe Smoothie 91
Avocado Maple Smoothie 92
Spicy Vegetable Smoothie 93
Kale Smoothie 95
Vanilla Yam Smoothie 96
Sweet Potato Banana Smoothie 97
Banana Kale Orange Smoothie 98
Eat Your Vegetables Smoothie 99

TOFU SMOOTHIES 100
Chocolate Tofu Smoothie 100
Banana Berry Tofu Smoothie 101
Apple Strawberry Banana Smoothie 102
Apple Peach Banana Smoothie 103
Banana Raspberry Tofu Smoothie 104

5 DAY SAMPLE MENU 105
Day One 107
Day Two 108
Day Three 109
Day Four 110
Day Five 111

SECTION 2: SMOOTHIE DIET 112
Common Smoothie Ingredients: 113

LIVER DETOX AND YOU 115

SMOOTHIES AND WEIGHT LOSS 119
Benefits of Soy Milk 120

PART 1: FRUIT SMOOTHIES 123
Recipe #1. The Basic Fruit Smoothie: 124
Recipe #2: The Frozen Banana Smoothie 126
Recipe #3: The Banana Berry Colada 128

Recipe #4: The Basic Grape Smoothie 130
Recipe #5: Raspberry-Orange Smoothie 132
Recipe #6: Kiwi-Apple Smoothie 134
Recipe #7: Apple-Lemon Smoothie 136
Recipe #8: Pear-Nut Smoothie 138
Recipe #9: Nutty Creamy Apple Smoothie 140
Recipe #10: Apple-Blueberry Smoothie 142
Recipe #11: Cherry Apple Smoothie 144
Recipe #12: CranBananaSmoothie 146
Recipe #13: Plum-Apple-LemonSmoothie 148
Recipe #14: Plum-Banana Smoothie 150
Recipe #15: Kiwi-Banana Smoothie 151
Recipe #16: Kiwi-Mint Smoothie 153
Recipe #17: Cantaloupe Strawberry Smoothie 155
Recipe #18: Cantaloupe-Apple Smoothie 157
Recipe #19: Pumpkin-Apple Smoothie w/ Cinnamon 159
Recipe #20: Basic Sweet Grapefruit 161
Recipe #21: Watermelon-Banana Smoothie 163
Recipe #22: Watermelon-Pear Smoothie 165
Recipe #23: Tangerine-Coconut Smoothie 167
Recipe #24: Tangerine-Pineapple Smoothie 169
Recipe #25: Pineapple-Vanilla Smoothie 171

PART 2: GREEN SMOOTHIES 173

Recipe #1: Banana-Papaya Smoothie 176
Recipe #2: Dandelion Smoothie 177
Recipe #3: Romaine Lettuce and Avocado Smoothie 179
Recipe #4: Fuji-Apple Avocado Smoothie 180
Recipe #5: Rainbow-Chard Smoothie 182
Recipe #6: Spinach-Banana Smoothie 184
Recipe #7: Young Coconut-Pineapple Smoothie 185
Recipe #9: Bell Pepper-Avocado Smoothie 188
Recipe #10: Tomatocado 189
Recipe #11: Red 'n Green 191
Recipe #12: Celery-Banana Smoothie 192
Recipe #13: Kale-Banana Smoothie 193
Recipe #14: Blueberry-Spinach Smoothie 194
Recipe #15: Lovely Tomato 195
Recipe #16: Purple Rainbow 196
Recipe #17: The Monster 197

Recipe #18: Basic Green Smoothie 198
Recipe #19: Green Grape Smoothie 199
Recipe #20: Pomegranate-Blueberry 200
Recipe #21: Acai Special 201
Recipe #22: Cucumber-Pear 202
Recipe #23: Citrus Sweet Potato Smoothie 203
Recipe #24: Banana and Broccoli Smoothie 204
Recipe #25: Celery-Red Grape Smoothie 205
Recipe #26: Mango-Tomato Smoothie 206

PART 3: BREAKFAST SMOOTHIES 207

Recipe #1: Blueberry Banana 207
Recipe #2: Oatmeal-Strawberry Smoothie 209
Recipe #3: Basic Berry Smoothie 210
Recipe #4: Banana Crunch Smoothie 211
Recipe #5: Raspberry-Peach Smoothie 212
Recipe #6: Basic Protein Smoothie 213
Recipe #7: Cherry Vanilla Smoothie 214
Recipe #8: Basic Apricot Breakfast Smoothie 215
Recipe #9: Pomegranate Smoothie 216
Recipe #10: Coffee-Banana Tofu Smoothie 217

PART 4: ENERGY SMOOTHIES 218

Recipe #1: Basic Energy Smoothie 221
Recipe #2: All Day Energy Smoothie 222
Recipe #3: Blueberry-Soy Smoothie 223
Recipe #4: Super Energy Smoothie 224
Recipe #5: Cocoa-Peanut Butter Smoothie 225

THE FIVE DAY MEAL PLAN 226

Introduction

Why go on a superfood smoothie diet? Smoothies are a great way to lose weight and to catapult you into a healthier dieting lifestyle. Superfoods are highly nutritious and can help the body to both treat and prevent health conditions like heart disease, diabetes, and even cancer. The nutrient in the superfoods is easily assimilated by the body by eating them rather than having to take supplements. If you get sick you may have to go on prescription medications and don't you think it is healthier to first prevent this from happening through your diet? Nature knows how to take proper care of the body if we allow it. Superfoods are easy to find in every grocery store and they are cost effective, especially if you consider the doctor bills you will save if you just stay healthy.

A healthy person can increase their chances of staying healthy and grow even stronger by going on a superfood smoothie diet. If a person has any health issue, they may can turn it around by going on the diet. It is a great "side effect" of the diet to help overcome certain health conditions. Some health conditions if left unchecked can be very grave in the outcome. It is as simple as eating healthy to help prevent a heart attack. Just knowing that alone should encourage more people to change their diets to a better healthier one.

What is it about superfoods that help our body to treat and prevent ill health conditions? It is because of the nutrients packed in the superfoods, nutrients like anti-oxidants. Beta carotene, vitamin A, C, E and selenium are anti-oxidants and so are CoQ10, ligand, lycopene, flavonoids, lutein, and polyphenols which are all found in abundance in superfoods. These nutrients are responsible for helping the body to build strong bones, strong immune system, which helps to fight off bad infections caused from free radicals.

Superfoods include many different food choices, which make going on the superfood diets so easy because you have a big variety to choose from for your meals. It does not matter which of the superfoods you eat, you can gain the nutrients from all of them. So if there is one you do not particularly care for you can eat of the other choices. You will not find as high a quality of the nutrients derived from the superfoods on any processed foods because you cannot spray on nutrients and it be the same as what nature provides. Nature provides the highest in quality of nutrients in the food.

The list of superfoods includes chocolate, tea, tomatoes, walnuts, yogurt, spinach, beans, kale, pumpkin, oranges, blueberries, broccoli, salmon, turkey, and oats. Most of the recipes within this book will call for these ingredients. If they are not in the recipes, you should include them with your meal plans.

You can find good protein as well as nutrients in fish. Cold water fish like salmon, mackerel, sardines, and herring contain high levels of omega 3 fatty acids and give the diet a well-rounded dose of nutrients. Omega 3 fatty acids are beneficial in fighting high cholesterol, brain issues, arthritis, and heart disease. You should include fish in your menu at least two or three times a week, but no more than that. Omega 3 fatty acids are also found in walnuts, eggs, and flax seeds.

You also need to include plenty of fiber in your diet, which works well along with the superfoods. Even some of the superfoods are also high in fiber like beans, fruits and vegetables, but it is good to include extra fiber in the menu. Fiber helps with weight loss too because it helps the body to feel full faster stopping you from eating more. Other foods high in fiber are whole grains.

Help the body to be even stronger and add calcium to your diet. Dairy foods including yogurt (which is a superfood) are high in calcium. Calcium helps to strengthen the bones. Bone issues are common with older adults and they need the calcium. It helps as a preventative to make sure you get plenty of calcium before the bones are brittle. But it can be a good treatment as well.

Chocolate is a favorite of many. The wonderful fact about chocolate and dark chocolate in particular is that it is a superfood and high in anti-oxidants. Many people struggle with a chocolate addiction and perhaps you do not have to give it all up. If you love it, have a little, because a little will give you some very beneficial nutrients.

A diet of superfoods will give your body a huge boost in helping it to be and stay healthy and strong. The nutrients in the superfoods are like giving your immune system muscles to fight off damage caused by free radicals and it even helps the body to treat and prevent conditions like high cholesterol, high blood pressure, and high blood sugar. Superfoods are safe for the whole family to consume because they are the best foods from nature. All the recipes in this book contain ingredients that include most of the superfoods listed above. All the recipes are delicious and nutritious and the smoothies offer a great way to lose weight.

Before going on the superfoods smoothie diet make sure you check with your health care provider. Go over the diet plan and make sure your body can handle a smoothie diet. You may wish to go on a complete smoothie diet and drink smoothies for all your meals and snacks, or go on a modified smoothie diet and include solid foods in with the plan. Ask your health care provider about adding exercise to your routine too especially if weight loss is your goal. Dieting and exercise are two of the best ways to lose weight fast and effectively. Make up your mind once you lose the weight to continue to eat superfoods to help manage your weight and health.

Section 1: Smoothie Diet Cookbook

Smoothies are a delicious way of enjoying nature's best in fruits and vegetables. They are a great way to eat a meal in a glass, offering a fast and easy means to preparing and eating. Many people today do not get enough proper nutrition due to busy lifestyles and fast convenient foods are their mainstay. A smoothie offers a fast and convenient way to consume fresh fruits and vegetables without the added preservatives and processed sugars. Even if a person does not like the taste of vegetables, the smoothie will be covered by the flavor of the added fruit, making it easy and pleasant to consume the food.

A smoothie is a drink created from fresh fruits and vegetables with a liquid, from either water or diary or something similar. Other flavors and textures can be added if desired and it helps to make the smoothie a complete meal to add proteins.

The Benefits of a Smoothie Diet, Fruits in Particular

The smoothies included on the smoothie diet are high in nutrients. It gives the body a good amount of vitamins and minerals and even healthful essential fatty acids when certain ingredients are included. This combination is a good way to receive the nutrients necessary to give the body energy. It takes energy to be able to move about and moving about, or exercising, is vital to a healthy body. If the desire it so lose weight, then exercising while going on the diet will help to facilitate both weight and fat loss. Smoothies offer a way to gain all the nutrients necessary in one glass, making it an easy diet to follow without a lot of prep work.

Being dehydrated is a major concern for some people. They do not take the time needed to drink the water their body needs each day. Or they drink junk food drinks that do not give the body any nutritional benefit. Being on the smoothie diet insures the body will stay well hydrated, since the smoothies are primarily liquid created from healthy foods like fruits and vegetables. Even if the main liquid of the smoothie is milk or yogurt, those are primarily made from water, so the body derives plenty of water from the drinks.

Many smoothie recipes contain dairy foods, which makes the smoothie recipe high in calcium. Calcium is a vital nutrient and is responsible for helping the body to have strong bones. Adding milk to the recipes helps to add this nutrient to the body. When the recipe calls for yogurt, there are added benefits in the form of good probiotics, which aids the digestive system. Using whole dairy over low fat will provide a higher level of the nutrients.

The smoothie diet is one of the easiest diets to create and follow. It does not take rocket science to concoct smoothie recipes and pour them into a glass to drink. It takes significantly less time than it does to prepare food and cook a meal. Adding ingredients to the smoothies allows the offering of extra nutrients. Adding a tablespoon of extra virgin coconut oil gives a good dose of healthy fatty acids as well as antioxidants.

Breakfast is the most important meal of the day. This meal gives the energy to face the rest of the day. If we eat junk for breakfast, the result will be a sluggish feeling, and weight gain. If we eat a nutritious meal we will have energy to burn, we will want to get up and move around. Often, breakfast is overlooked due to time restraints. Busy lifestyles have us getting up late and running, unable to stop and cook a healthy breakfast. A smoothie for breakfast makes it possible to have a nutritious and quick breakfast. It only takes a few minutes to fix and drink. Much of the ingredients can be prepped the night before, so it will be ready to go the morning of. Some smoothies will allow for fixing ahead of time and storage in the refrigerator.

One of the best breakfast foods are fruit. These are packed with nutrients and have enough sweetness to them to satisfy our sweet tooth. By pairing fruit with nutritious oils and dairy, the result is a drink that will give the body energy and satisfaction. No hunger pangs, just a good feeling of wellness. Pick and choose ingredients that offer the highest level of nutrition and ones that work well together to help give the body an energy boost, which is the most important aspect of a breakfast food.

Most of the smoothie recipes do contain fruit a few contain vegetables. Fruits are high in carbohydrates. Good carbs are what gives the body the energy needed to move. Fruits contain natural sweeteners, which the body assimilates faster and easier than processed sweeteners. Caution should be made when looking to drink a prepackage smoothie over one that is home made. Prepackaged smoothies may contain added sugar and calories, which will not facilitate weight and fat loss, but will instead add to it.

The smoothie diets give the body a high amount of antioxidants, which are vital nutrients. Antioxidants are vitamins like A, C and E. These help the body to fight off free radicals. Free radicals are agents that attack the cells in the body and can lead to detrimental diseases like cancer. If the body has enough of these antioxidants, it can fight off these illnesses because it boosts and strengthens the immune system.

In addition to antioxidants, healthy smoothies also contain high levels of vital vitamins and minerals that come from the fresh foods added. All fruit is healthy, containing good levels of vitamins and minerals. Each fruit varies in the content of the nutrition; it helps to include a big variety of fruits while on the smoothie diet. For example, oranges and strawberries contain vitamin C. Cantaloupe, papaya, and peaches contain vitamin A, and B vitamins are found in bananas and cantaloupes. Bananas are known for containing potassium. Ever hear of the advice to eat a banana to keep from getting muscle spasms? Cantaloupe also contains potassium. Copper is found in kiwi, peaches, and pineapple. Bananas, blueberries, and strawberries contain manganese.

Fiber is a valuable substance in food for the body. Without fiber the body would stop up, the digestive system would become sluggish and unable to absorb all the nutrients needed to be healthy. Fruit provides a natural source high in fiber, especially if the peels and skins of the fruit are eaten (like pears, apples and even on berries.) The meat of the fruit also contains fiber, especially kiwi, bananas and papayas and even cherries and strawberries. When eating a healthy smoothie diet be ready for a good digestive system cleanse.

A good healthy smoothie needs an added protein because fruit by itself is not too high in protein. Adding dairy, like milk or yogurt helps to provide the needed protein. Even a spoon of powdered milk will give the smoothie a nice protein boost. Protein is needed along with carbohydrates to help the body. While the carbs give energy, proteins give the cells substance, to build muscles, to move.

One of the major benefits of the smoothie diet is the low fat content in the food. Some fat is needed, so do not feel bad by choosing to use whole dairy foods. However, if you want to go lowest possible fat, choose the low fat versions of milk and yogurts.

The Benefits of Drinking Green Smoothies

Not all smoothies are made with fruit only. There is a line of smoothies that add vegetables, in particular, green veggies, thus the term "green smoothies." Going on the smoothie diet insures the body will get plenty of fruit, which is good because as discovered above, fruit contains many good nutrient. However, vegetables are just as good and contains added nutrients, some even higher in antioxidants than fruits. Many people though may turn their nose up at the thought of drinking a pureed vegetable, thinking it will not taste good. Or perhaps they feel only the diehard nutrition 'freaks' are the only ones to drink such smoothies. But the truth is vegetables are a great addition to the ingredient list for smoothie recipes. They do add their own flavors, but often, the fruit and dairy will overpower the vegetable. This allows the benefit of eating their vegetables but only tasting the fruits.

Raw vegetables are the most nutritious. When we cook vegetables, they lose some of their nutrition. Since creating smoothies requires raw ingredients, the nutrition derived from vegetables is high. The benefits of drinking a diet smoothie made with vegetables are powerful. Again, there are pre-packaged green smoothies, but often the veggies included in these are processed and pasteurized, and this causes the vegetable to lose its nutritional benefits. It is better to stick with making all smoothies from scratch to derive the most nutrition.

The diets of today, or lack of good diet, means that people are not gaining the full benefit from the foods they eat. If a person eats a lot of processed foods and junk foods, then it is likely they are not receiving any fresh fruits and vegetables. This causes a host of problems in the body starting with deficiencies of the essential vitamins and minerals we need in order to stay healthy. People think they can gain their nutrients from swallowing supplements, but the benefit is not the same. The best way for the body to get these vital nutrients are from eating highly nutritious whole foods, mainly from fruits and vegetables. Consuming green smoothies, smoothies with vegetables gives the body added vitamin A, B, C and K as well as folate, fiber, omega 3 fatty acids, iron, and zinc.

Vegetables help with weight loss and maintenance. The added vegetables in the smoothies makes them more satisfying and thus people are not as hunger after consuming them and are able to make it to their next snack or meal without being too hungry in between. A really good green smoothie will have sixty-percent fruit with forty percent vegetables. This combination makes the food easier to digest and the body gains the benefit of the nutrients as a result. Junk foods go through the body faster and thus hunger comes on faster, but also because of junk food, the body is not able to absorb all the nutrients from the foods. Eating fruits and vegetables, especially in raw form, slows down the digestive process just enough that the body is able to absorb all the proper nutrients. It also gives a fuller feeling longer, curbing the hunger and stopping the need to graze and snack. In essence, the more junk food you eat, the hungrier you will be and you will keep eating more to try to satisfy the hunger.

Smoothies are actually very good to taste. This is why so many enjoy making smoothies for quickie breakfasts and snacks regardless of their main diet. So many people do not like the taste of vegetables and smoothies, especially green smoothies, given the opportunity to include vegetables without the worry of the taste hindering the enjoyment of it. Because smoothies are more fruit, the fruit flavor overpowers the vegetable flavor.

Lose Weight and Fat on the Smoothie Diet

The smoothie diet makes it easy to lose weight and body fat because of the ease in both the creation of smoothies and the ease of drinking them. It is almost too easy, but once a person starts the smoothie diet and sees how easy it is they may have to force themselves to eat whole foods again.

If you eat smoothies for each meal, you will want to try to incorporate more protein by adding protein powder (found at health food stores). A spoon or two of this and it makes the smoothie a complete meal. Feel free to add extra foods to the recipes, if you want the recipe sweeter, try throwing in some extra ripe pieces of fruits, especially berries, will add to the sweetness factor.

Smoothie Creations - A Quick How To Guide

The star of the smoothie creation is the blender. You cannot make a decent smoothie without one, so if you do not have one, go purchase one. You can use a food processor too if that is all you have. You will want a decent blender, one that will be able to handle pureeing whole pieces of fruit and vegetables.

Fresh fruit and vegetables are always the best, however, frozen will work just as well. Sometimes fresh fruits and vegetables may not be available, so you will have to turn to frozen. Canned fruits and vegetables can work in a pinch, but only if you absolutely cannot find them in fresh or frozen form. Remember canned foods are processed and cooked and have lost some of their nutrients in the process.

Some fruits and maybe a few vegetables may contain enough juice to create a good smoothie, providing all the liquid needed. However, some do not and the addition of a liquid is needed. Many smoothie recipes call for milk or yogurt. Some may use water and some may use a dairy substitute. This gives some protein in the mix as well. Other "liquid" choices include nut milks, tea, actual fruit juice, ice cream, yogurt, sparkling water, and plain water.

If you are on a smoothie diet and drinking them with every meal or in place of every meal, you will want to sprinkle protein powder in the mix. Protein powder is made from soy, rice, and whey.

A well-balanced smoothie meal will have fruit, vegetables, and protein. Even if you are making one of the fruit only recipes, you can add some sneaky vegetables into the mix and no one will be the wiser. Sneak in a bit of chopped spinach or kale. Try some celery or even beetroot. If you cannot find fresh vegetables, visit your local health food store and purchase green plant powder, and add a spoonful of this to turn the fruit smoothie into a green smoothie.

If you want the smoothie to taste sweeter instead of grabbing for the sugar bowl try some of these suggestions: a ripe banana, a spoonful or two of honey, stevia, or agave nectar.

Do you want to spice up the smoothie or give it more flavor? Try adding some extra ingredients that add a burst of flavor like vanilla extract, cayenne pepper, almond extract, coconut milk, cinnamon, salt, or a spoonful of nut butter.

If you enjoy a thicker and colder smoothie try crushing ice and including it in the blender. Only do this when you plan to drink the smoothie right then. You cannot store smoothies with ice chunks for too long in the refrigerator or the smoothie will be too thin and runny. Some smoothies may be good as frozen pops, experiment with this, especially if it is hot weather, and if you enjoy frozen pops.

If your blender is new, you may need to experiment with the settings to figure out which ones will work best for the smoothie recipes. Sometimes you may need to puree to get the desired texture, while other times just the blend setting will work.

Just because you are on the smoothie diet does not mean you cannot enjoy whole foods too. If you have made a smoothie using berries, save a few for garnishment once the smoothie is done. You can also garnish with a different fruit or even a wedge of lemon or a mint sprig or parsley leaf (depending on whether or not the smoothie is sweet or savory.)

Tips for Making Good Smoothies

If you find you have a fruit or vegetable that is difficult to blend into a drink, try "juicing" it first. You will need a juicer in order to do this. Juicers are able to handle turning even the toughest pieces of fruit and vegetables into a liquid. If you do not own a juicer, try peeling the fruit or vegetable first. Blend the center first. Chop the peel into fine pieces and add it a little bit at a time until the smoothie is at the consistency you desire. Always chop the fruit and vegetables before adding to the blender.

If the smoothie is too thin, try adding a bit more fruit, or ice cubes. If it is too thick, thin it with liquid, milk, yogurt, ice cream, or even fruit juice or water. If you wish for a creamy smoothie use yogurt or ice cream for the liquid instead of water and ice.

It is okay to refrigerate or even freeze a smoothie if you cannot consume it right after creating it. Allow a frozen smoothie to thaw in the refrigerator for a day, or allow it to sit out at room temperature for about an hour. If you refrigerate it, drink it within a day.

If you plan to use fruit juice for the liquid try freezing it in ice trays first, that way it will help the smoothie to have a thicker frozen texture.

When blending the smoothie always test a spoonful first to make sure of the flavor and texture before pouring into a glass.

Note: Most of the recipes within this book are for 1 serving, since these types of diets are normally enjoyed by one person at a time. It is easy to double or triple or more each recipe as needed. Always peel bananas and discard the peel. Always cut the leaves from the fruit, such as the tops of strawberries.

Measurement Help: 1 banana equals 1/3 cup.

Fruit Smoothies

Peanut Banana Berry Smoothie

A nutritious smoothie that provides omega 3 fatty acids from flax seed meal.

Makes 1 serving.

Ingredients:

*1/2 cup of milk
*1/4 cup of banana (ripe)
*1/4 cup of blueberries (fresh or frozen)
*1/4 cup of yogurt (plain)
*1/2 tablespoon of flax seed meal
*1/2 tablespoon of peanut butter
*1/2 teaspoon of honey

Directions:

First, grind the 1/2 tablespoon of flax seed meal into a fine powder. Next, add the 1/2 cup of milk, 1/4 cup of ripe banana, 1/4 cup of blueberries, 1/4 cup of plain yogurt, 1/2 tablespoon of peanut butter and the 1/2 teaspoon of honey into a blender and blend until the texture you desire. Pour into a glass and enjoy.

Blackberry Banana Smoothie

It is hard to beat the sweet flavor of fresh ripe blackberries (or frozen if they are not in season).

Makes 1 serving.

Ingredients:

*1/2 cup of ice (crushed)
*1/4 cup of blackberries (fresh is best, but frozen will work) + 3 whole blackberries
*1/4 cup of banana (ripe)
*1/8 cup of orange juice
*2 strawberries
*1/4 teaspoon of honey

Directions:

Add the 1/2 cup of crushed ice, 1/4 cup of blackberries, 1/4 cup of ripe banana, 1/4 cup of orange juice, and the 1/4 teaspoon of honey. Cut the top off the strawberries and cut them in half, add to the blender. Blend until smooth. Pour into a glass and garnish with the 3 blackberries.

Spicy Banana Smoothie

Here is a banana smoothie with some spice from cinnamon and a bit of nuttiness from almond butter.

Makes 1 serving.

Ingredients:

*1 banana
*1 1/2 cups of almond milk
*1/4 cup of almond butter
*2 tablespoons of honey
*1 tablespoon of cinnamon (ground)

Directions:

PREP: First, freeze the banana, and then once frozen, peel and chop it into bits.

Once the banana is prepared, pour the 1 1/2 cups of almond milk into the blender and add the 1/4 cup of almond butter, 2 tablespoons of honey, and the tablespoon of ground cinnamon. Blend until smooth, then add the chopped frozen banana and blend until the texture you desire. Pour into a glass and enjoy.

Watermelon Banana Berry Smoothie

There is nothing quite as refreshing as this smoothie, it is best made in the summer when the watermelons are plentiful and sweet.

Makes 1 serving.

Ingredients:

*1/2 cup of cranberry juice
*1/2 cup of strawberries
*1/4 cup of blueberries
*1/4 cup of watermelon (chunked)
*1/4 cup of banana (ripe)
*1/2 of a fig

Directions:

Add the 1/2 cup of cranberry juice to a blender along with the 1/2 cup of strawberries, 1/4 cup of blueberries, 1/4 cup of chunked watermelon, 1/4 cup of ripe banana and the 1/2 fig. Blend until it reaches desired texture. Pour into a glass and enjoy.

Mango Papaya Smoothie

Mango paired with papaya and mixed with orange and lime makes for a delicious tropical smoothie.

Makes 1 serving.

Ingredients:

*1/2 cup of water
*1/8 cup of papaya (peeled and diced)
*1/8 cup of mango (sliced)
*1/8 cup of orange juice
*1/2 tablespoon of lime juice
*1/2 tablespoon of honey
*1/8 teaspoon of orange zest
*glass of crushed ice

Directions:

First step, add the 1/8 cup of peeled, diced papaya and the 1/8 cup of sliced mango into the blender. Puree. Add the 1/8 cup of orange juice, 1/2 tablespoon of lime juice, 1/2 tablespoon of honey and 1/8 teaspoon of orange zest and blend until smooth. Pour over the crushed ice and enjoy.

Banana Coconut Smoothie

This tropical smoothie is extra sweet with ice cream.

Makes 1 serving.

Ingredients:

*1 1/2 scoop of vanilla ice cream
*1 banana (ripe)
*1/2 cup of coconut milk
*1 teaspoon of honey

Directions:

Add the 1 1/2 scoops of vanilla ice cream along with the ripe banana, 1/2 cup of coconut milk and teaspoon of honey to a blender. Blend until smooth. Pour into glass and enjoy.

Fruit Spread Smoothie

This smoothie uses 2 tablespoons of your favorite all natural fruit spread. Fruit spread is not just for bread! Makes 1 serving.

Ingredients:

*1/2 cup of milk
*1/4 cup of yogurt (plain)
*1/4 cup of strawberries (fresh or frozen, sliced)
*2 tablespoons of all-natural fruit spread (your favorite flavor)
*1 tablespoon of oats

Directions:

Add the 1/2 cup of milk, 1/4 cup of plain yogurt, 1/4 cup of sliced strawberries, 2 tablespoons of your favorite all-natural fruit spread and 1 tablespoon of oats to the blender. Blend until it reaches desired consistency. Pour in a glass and enjoy.

Nothing But Fruit Smoothie

The thing that sets this smoothie a part from others is the presence of nothing but fruit in the mix.

Makes 1 serving.

Ingredients:

*1/3 cup of banana (chunked)
*1/2 cup of strawberries (frozen)
*1/2 cup of blueberries (frozen)
*1/2 cup of pineapple juice

Directions:

First, pour the 1/2 cup of pineapple juice in the blender and add the 1/3 cup of chunked bananas. Blend until smooth. Add the 1/2 cup of frozen strawberries and the 1/2 cup of frozen blueberries and blend until desired texture is achieved. Pour into glass and enjoy.

Creamy Strawberry Smoothie

Strawberries are the star of this delicious creamy smoothie.

Makes 1 serving.

Ingredients:

*1/4 cup of milk
*1/4 cup of yogurt (plain)
*4 strawberries
*3 ice cubes (crushed)
*1 1/2 tablespoons of honey
*1 teaspoon of vanilla extract

Directions:

Add the 1/4 cup of milk, 1/4 cup of plain yogurt, 4 strawberries, 3 crushed ice cubes, 1 1/2 tablespoons of honey, and teaspoon of vanilla extract into a blender and blend until smooth. Pour into a glass and enjoy.

Apple Spice Smoothie

This smoothie is made from applesauce, making it extra creamy.

Makes 1 serving.

Ingredients:

*1 cup of applesauce
*1/2 cup of apple cider
*1/2 cup of orange juice
*1 tablespoon of maple syrup
*1/4 teaspoon of nutmeg (ground)
*1/4 teaspoon of cinnamon (ground)

Directions:

Add the 1 cup of applesauce in a blender along with the 1/2 cup of apple cider, 1/2 cup of orange juice, tablespoon of maple syrup, 1/4 teaspoon of ground nutmeg, and the 1/4 teaspoon of ground cinnamon. Blend until smooth and serve in a glass.

Banana Berry Vanilla Smoothie

A delicious and creamy banana and blueberry smoothies.

Makes 1 serving.

Ingredients:

*1 cup of soy milk (vanilla)
*3/4 cup of bananas (sliced)
*1/2 cup of blueberries (frozen)
*1/2 cup of yogurt (vanilla)

Directions:

Prep: Slice the banana (after peeling) and freeze the slices.

In a blender, add the 1 cup of vanilla soy milk, 3/4 cup of frozen sliced bananas, 1/2 cup of frozen blueberries, and the 1/2 cup of vanilla yogurt. Blend well and pour into a glass and serve.

Refreshing Smoothie

This smoothie is refreshing with a taste of lemon in the mix.

Makes 1 serving.

Ingredients:

*1 cup of yogurt (vanilla)
*1/4 cup of banana (chunked)
*3 strawberries (cut up and frozen)
*1/2 tablespoon of honey
*1/4 teaspoon of vanilla extract
*1/4 teaspoon of lemon juice
*ice

Directions:

Add the cup of vanilla yogurt, 1/4 cup of chunked banana, 3 cut up and frozen strawberries, 1/2 tablespoon of honey, 1/4 teaspoon of vanilla extract, and 1/4 teaspoon of lemon juice in a blender and blend well. Add enough ice and blend more to get the smoothie to the texture you desire. Pour in a glass and enjoy.

Peachy Banana Berry Vanilla Smoothie

The flavors dance on the palate, bananas, orange, vanilla, peach and strawberry.

Makes 1 serving.

Ingredients:

*3/4 cup of yogurt (vanilla)
*1/2 cup of strawberries (frozen)
*1/3 cup of peaches (frozen)
*1/4 cup of banana
*1/2 tablespoon of orange juice (from frozen concentrate can)

In a blender add the 3-4 cup of vanilla yogurt, 1/2 cup of frozen strawberries, 1/3 cup of frozen peaches, 1/4 cup of bananas and the 1/2 tablespoon of frozen orange juice concentrate and blend until smooth. Pour in a glass and enjoy.

Extra Large Fruit Punch Smoothie

This is a delightful smoothie created with all the fun fruits of summer.

Makes one extra-large serving, or 2 small servings.

Ingredients:

*1/2 cup of ice
*1/2 cup of ice cream (vanilla)
*1/3 cup of strawberries (frozen)
*1/3 cup of all natural fruit punch
*1/4 cup of banana
*1/4 cup of peach nectar
*1 strawberry sliced (garnishment)

In a blender, add the 1/2 cup of ice, 1/2 cup of vanilla ice cream, 1/3 cup of frozen strawberries, 1/3 cup of all natural fruit punch, 1/4 cup of bananas, 1/4 cup of peach nectar and blend until smooth consistency. Pour into a tall glass and garnish with strawberry slices if desired.

Raspberry Banana Smoothie

Enjoy this smoothie lightly flavored with frozen raspberries and bananas.

Makes 1 serving.

*3/4 cup of almond milk (sweetened)
*1/2 cup of frozen raspberries
*1/2 cup of yogurt (vanilla)
*1/4 cup of banana (chunked and frozen)

In a blender, add the 3/4 cup of sweetened almond milk, 1/2 cup of frozen raspberries, 1/2 cup of vanilla yogurt, and the 1/4 cup of chunked frozen bananas and blend until smooth. Pour in glass and enjoy.

Mango Banana Smoothie

A unique and delicious combination with the mango and banana.

Makes 1 serving.

Ingredients:

*1/2 cup of yogurt (vanilla)
*1/2 cup of orange juice (fresh squeezed)
*1/4 cup of banana
*1 mango

Peel and remove the pit in the mango. Chop it, put into a blender along with the 1/2 cup of vanilla yogurt, 1/2 cup of fresh squeezed orange juice, and the 1/4 cup of banana, and blend until smooth. Pour into a glass and enjoy.

Vanilla Orange Banana Smoothie

A delicious cream sickle flavored smoothie.

Makes 1 extra-large serving.

Ingredients:

*1/2 cup of yogurt (vanilla)
*1/2 cup of orange juice (fresh squeezed)
*1/2 cup of ice
*1/4 cup of milk
*1/4 cup of banana
*2 tablespoons of honey

Add the 1/2 cup of vanilla yogurt, 1/2 cup of fresh squeezed orange juice, 1/2 cup of ice, 1/4 cup of milk, 1/4 cup of bananas along with the 2 tablespoons of honey in a blender and blend until smooth. Pour in a glass and enjoy.

Purple Smoothie

Purple in color from the mix of red strawberries, orange and blue from blueberries.

Makes 1 serving.

Ingredients:

*1/2 cup of yogurt (plain)
*1/4 cup of strawberries
*1/8 cup of blueberries (frozen)
*1/8 cup of bananas (chunked)
*1/8 cup of orange juice
*1/4 tablespoon of soy milk powder

Directions:

Add the 1/2 cup of plain yogurt, 1/4 cup of strawberries, 1/8 cup of frozen blueberries, 1/8 cup of chunked bananas, 1/8 cup of orange juice and the 1/4 tablespoon of soy milk powder to a blender and blend until smooth. Pour in a glass and enjoy.

Fruit Milky Smoothie

A very simple smoothie with four simple ingredients, this is a can't go wrong recipe.

Makes 1 serving.

*1/2 cup of apples (chopped, peeled and cored)
*1/4 cup of orange juice
*1/8 cup of bananas (frozen chopped)
*1/8 cup of milk

Directions:

Chop the apple into fine chunks and add 1/2 cup to a blender along with 1/4 cup of orange juice, 1/8 cup of frozen chopped bananas, and 1/8 cup of milk. Blend until smooth and pour into a glass to serve.

Strawberry Pear Smoothie

A perfect smoothie to enjoy when the fruit harvest comes through in the summer.

Makes 1 serving.

Ingredients:

*1/2 of a pair (cubed and cored)
*1/3 cup of yogurt (vanilla)
*1/4 cup of ice
*1/8 cup of milk
*1 strawberry
*1 teaspoon of honey

Directions:

Add the 1/4 cup of ice in the bottom of the blender then add the 1/2 of a cubed pear, along with the 1/3 cup of vanilla yogurt, 1/8 cup of milk, hulled strawberry and the teaspoon of honey. Blend until smooth, pour into a glass, and enjoy.

Spicy Banana Smoothie

Combine the flavors of banana with orange, raspberry and nutmeg and enjoy the flavor explosion in your mouth.

Makes 1 serving.

Ingredients:

*1/4 cup of yogurt (raspberry)
*1/4 cup of bananas (chunked and frozen)
*1/4 cup of an orange (chopped and peeled)
*1/2 tablespoon of honey
*1/8 teaspoon of nutmeg (ground)

Directions:

In a blender, add the 1/4 cup of raspberry yogurt with the 1/4 cup of chunked frozen bananas, 1/4 cup of chopped, peeled orange, 1/2 tablespoon of honey and 1/8 teaspoon of ground nutmeg and blend until smooth. Pour into a glass and enjoy.

PB Banana Smoothie

This is a delightful smoothie that combines the wonderful flavor of peanut butter with banana to bring the timeless classic combination to a smoothie.

Makes 1 serving.

Ingredients:

*1/4 cup of milk
*1/4 cup of banana (chunked)
*1/8 cup of peanut butter (creamy)
*1 tablespoon of honey
*3 ice cubes

Directions:

Add the 1/4 cup of milk into a blender along with 1/4 cup of chunked banana, 1/8 cup of creamy peanut butter, tablespoon of honey and 3 ice cubes and blend until smooth. Pour in glass and serve immediately.

Herbed Strawberry Mango Smoothie

This fruity smoothie comes complete with a basil kick.

Makes 1 serving.

Ingredients:

*5 strawberries (chopped)
*4 basil leaves (fresh)
*3 ice cubes
*1 cup of cold water
*1 cup of mango (frozen, chunked)
*2 tablespoons of honey

Directions:

Add the 5 chopped strawberries, 4 fresh basil leaves, cup of cold water, cup of frozen chunked mango to the blender and blend. Add the 3 ice cubes and 2 tablespoons of honey and blend for a few more seconds to disperse the ice. Pour into a glass and enjoy.

Orange Berry All Fruit Smoothie

This refreshing smoothie makes a great snack or dessert.

Makes 1 serving.

Ingredients:

*3/4 cup of strawberries (frozen)
*1/4 cup of orange juice
*1 tablespoon of raspberries (frozen)

Directions:

Blend the 3/4 cup of frozen strawberries, 1/4 cup of orange juice, and the 1 tablespoon of frozen raspberries until smooth. Pour into a glass and enjoy.

Berry Berry Smoothie

Berries are everywhere in this delicious, all berry smoothie, which makes for a great snack.

Makes 1 serving.

Ingredients:

*1 cup of berries (you choose, mix them up- raspberries, strawberries, blackberries)
*5 ice cubes
*1/8 cup of water
*1/8 cup of all berry all natural fruit juice
*1/8 cup of raspberries (frozen)
*1/8 cup of blueberries (frozen)

Directions:

Add the 5 ice cubes to the blender and crush before adding the 1/8 cup of cold water and the 1/8 cup of berry juice. Blend a few seconds then add the cup of mixed berries along with the 1/8 cup of frozen raspberries and the 1/8 cup of frozen blueberries, blend until smooth, and serve immediately.

Blueberry Banana Protein Smoothie

This is a good meal replacement smoothie because of the added protein powder, blueberry and banana flavor.

Makes 1 serving.

Ingredients:

*1/2 cup of soymilk (vanilla)
*1/2 cup of blueberries (frozen)
*1/4 cup of bananas (chunked and frozen)
*1/4 cup of ice cubes
*1/2 tablespoon of soy protein powder
*1/2 teaspoon of honey

Directions:

Add the 1/2 cup of soymilk (vanilla), 1/2 cup of blueberries (frozen), 1/4 cup of bananas (chunked and frozen), 1/4 cup of ice cubes, 1/2 tablespoon of soy protein powder, and the 1/2 teaspoon of honey to a blender and blend until smooth. Pour in a glass and enjoy.

Mango Blueberry Smoothie

A delicious smoothie strong on mango and blueberry flavor with a hint of vanilla.

Makes 1 serving.

Ingredients:

*1/2 cup of yogurt (vanilla)
*1/2 cup of mango juice
*1/4 cup of blueberries (frozen)
*1/4 cup of mango (frozen chunks)
*1 tablespoon of chia seeds (fine ground)
*1/2 teaspoon of vanilla extract

Directions:

Add the 1/2 cup of yogurt (vanilla), 1/2 cup of mango juice, 1/4 cup of blueberries (frozen), 1/4 cup of mango (frozen chunks), 1 tablespoon of chia seeds (fine ground), and the 1/2 teaspoon of vanilla extract into a blender and blend until smooth. Pour into a glass and enjoy.

Tapioca Chai Smoothie

This smoothie needs a spoon to enjoy the tapioca pearls.

Makes 1 serving.

Ingredients:

*1 cup of ice
*1/2 cup of tapioca pearls
*1/2 cup of milk
*1/2 cup of chai tea (mix)
*1 1/2 tablespoon of honey (divided)

Directions:

Prep: In a small saucepan, add water to fill half the pan. Turn heat to high and bring water to a boil. Add the 1/2 cup of tapioca pearls and bring the water to a second boil, stirring continually. Place a lid on the saucepan, turn the heat to medium, and set timer for 45 minutes. Take the saucepan off the stove, but keep the lid on, allow to sit for an extra half an hour to cool. Pour the pearls out into a strainer and rinse under cool water. Place the tapioca in a bowl, drizzle the 1 tablespoon of honey over, and toss.

Pour the 1 cup of ice and 1/2 cup of milk into a blender along with the 1/2 cup of chai tea mix and 1/2 tablespoon of honey and blend until slushy. Pour the smoothie into a glass, then add the honey coated tapioca pearls and stir. Enjoy.

Refreshingly Fruity Smoothie

Enjoy the flavors of almond with cherry, banana and oranges in this smoothie.

Makes 1 serving.

Ingredients:

*1/2 cup of yogurt (cherry)
*1/2 cup of mandarin oranges
*1/4 cup of banana (chunked)
*1/8 cup of half-and-half cream
*1/2 teaspoon of almond extract
*1 cherry

Directions:

Add in a blender the 1/2 cup of yogurt (cherry), 1/2 cup of mandarin oranges, 1/4 cup of banana (chunked), 1/8 cup of half-and-half cream, and the 1/2 teaspoon of almond extract and blend until smooth. Pour into a glass and garnish with the cherry. Enjoy.

Cherry Lemon Banana Smoothie

What do you get when you combine lemon with cherries and bananas? This delicious smoothie.

Makes 1 serving.

Ingredients:

*1/2 cup of cherries (frozen and pitted)
*1/4 cup of banana (chunked)
*1/4 cup of Greek yogurt
*3 ice cubes
*lemon juice (from a piece of a quartered lemon)
*1/8 teaspoon of almond extract

Directions:

In a blender add the 1/2 cup of cherries (frozen and pitted), 1/4 cup of banana (chunked), 1/4 cup of Greek yogurt, 3 ice cubes, lemon juice (from a piece of a quartered lemon), and 1/8 teaspoon of almond extract and blend until smooth. Pour into a glass and enjoy.

Berry Good Cherry Smoothie

Cherries, raspberries and red grapes make this an extra sweet delicious smoothie.

Makes 1 serving.

Ingredients:

*1/3 cup of cherry juice
*1/3 cup of yogurt (vanilla)
*1/3 cup of raspberries (frozen)
*1/8 cup of grapes (red, seedless)
*1 teaspoon of honey

Directions:

Add in a blender 1/3 cup of cherry juice, 1/3 cup of yogurt (vanilla), 1/3 cup of raspberries (frozen), 1/8 cup of grapes (red, seedless), and 1 teaspoon of honey and blend until smooth. Pour in a glass and enjoy.

Hot Chocolate Strawberry Smoothie

Don't let the name fool you, this smoothie is plenty cool and strawberry, but starts with a nice shot of hot chocolate.

Makes 1 serving.

Ingredients:

*1 cup of milk
*4 tablespoons of strawberries (frozen)
*4 ice cubes
*2 teaspoons of cocoa powder
*1 teaspoon of honey
*1 teaspoon of hot water

Directions:

First, in a cup, mix the teaspoon of hot water with the 2 teaspoons of cocoa powder to make a smooth paste. Next, add the 1 cup of milk, 4 tablespoons of strawberries (frozen), 4 ice cubes, and the 1 teaspoon of honey in a blender and stir in the cocoa paste. Blend until smooth, pour in a glass and enjoy.

Hot Chocolate Blueberry Smoothie

Don't let the name fool you, this smoothie is plenty cool and blueberry, but starts with a nice shot of hot chocolate.

Makes 1 serving.

Ingredients:

*1 cup of milk
*4 tablespoons of blueberries (frozen)
*4 ice cubes
*2 teaspoons of cocoa powder
*1 teaspoon of honey
*1 teaspoon of hot water

Directions:

First, in a cup, *mix* the teaspoon of hot water with the 2 teaspoons of cocoa powder to make a smooth paste. Next, add the 1 cup of milk, 4 tablespoons of blueberries (frozen), 4 ice cubes, and the 1 teaspoon of honey in a blender and stir in the cocoa paste. Blend until smooth, pour in a glass and enjoy.

Banana Cherry Cordial Smoothie

This is certainly a delightful dessert or snack smoothie.

Makes 1 serving.

Ingredients:

*1/2 cup of cherries (pitted and frozen)
*1/2 cup of chocolate milk
*1/4 cup of bananas (frozen chunks)

Directions:

In a blender, add 1/2 cup of cherries (pitted and frozen), 1/2 cup of chocolate milk, and 1/4 cup of bananas (frozen chunks) and blend until smooth. Pour in a glass and enjoy.

Simple Chocolate Peanut Butter Banana Smoothie

All the flavors loved by so many wrapped into a delicious smoothie.

Makes 1 serving.

Ingredients:

*1/2 cup of milk
*1/4 cup of banana (chunked)
*2 tablespoons of peanut butter (creamy)
*2 tablespoons of chocolate syrup

Directions:

In a blender, add 1/2 cup of milk, 1/4 cup of banana (chunked), 2 tablespoons of peanut butter (creamy), and 2 tablespoons of chocolate syrup and blend until smooth. Pour in a glass and enjoy.

Acai Cinnamon Berry Smoothie

This smoothie packs a little more punch with the inclusion of egg whites in the mix.

Makes 1 serving.

Ingredients:

*1/2 cup of acai juice
*1/4 cup of strawberries (frozen)
*1/8 cup of pasteurized liquid egg whites
*1/8 cup of apple cider
*1 tablespoon of honey
*1/3 tablespoon of cocoa powder
*1/4 tablespoon of cinnamon (ground)
*1/4 teaspoon of turmeric

Directions:

In a blender add 1/2 cup of acai juice, 1/4 cup of strawberries (frozen), 1/8 cup of pasteurized liquid egg whites, 1/8 cup of apple cider, 1 tablespoon of honey, 1/3 tablespoon of cocoa powder, 1/4 tablespoon of cinnamon (ground), and 1/4 teaspoon of turmeric and blend until smooth. Pour in a glass and enjoy.

Spicy Pear Smoothie

A delightful variation with your favorite smoothie drinks with pears.

Makes 1 serving.

Ingredients:

*1 pear (cored and chunked)
*1/2 cup of milk
*1/4 cup of banana (chunked)
*1/4 cup of yogurt (vanilla)
*1 teaspoon of cinnamon (ground)
*shake of nutmeg (ground)

Directions:

In a blender, add 1 pear (cored and chunked), 1/2 cup of milk, 1/4 cup of banana (chunked), 1/4 cup of yogurt (vanilla), 1 teaspoon of cinnamon (ground), and shake of nutmeg (ground) and blend until smooth. Pour in a glass and enjoy.

Sweet Banana Nut Smoothie

Couple banana with coconut and you get this delicious and sweet smoothie.

Makes 1 serving.

Ingredients:

*1/2 cup of coconut milk
*1/2 cup of bananas (chunked)
*1 1/2 scoops of ice cream (vanilla)
*1 teaspoon of honey

Directions:

In a blender, add 1/2 cup of coconut milk, 1/2 cup of bananas (chunked), 1 1/2 scoops of ice cream (vanilla), and 1 teaspoon of honey and blend until smooth. Pour in a glass and enjoy.

Hot Chocolate Dessert Smoothie

This smoothie is too decadent to be called anything but a dessert.

Makes 1 serving.

Ingredients:

*1 1/2 cups of milk
*1 1/2 scoops of ice cream (vanilla)
*1/4 cup of whipped cream
*2 tablespoons of hot cocoa mix
*5 cookies (your favorite kind that goes well with chocolate - crushed)
*extra whipped topping
*extra crushed cookies

Directions:

In a blender add 1 1/2 cups of milk, 1 1/2 scoops of ice cream (vanilla), 1/4 cup of whipped cream, 2 tablespoons of hot cocoa mix , 5 cookies (crushed) and blend until smooth. Pour in a glass and enjoy. Garnish with whipped topping and a sprinkling of crushed cookies.

Orange Berry Banana Smoothie

This is a delicious combination of orange, cranberry, banana, strawberry and raspberry flavors.

Makes 1 servings.

Ingredients:

*1/2 cup of cranberry juice
*1/2 cup of ice cubes
*1/4 cup of banana (chunked)
*1/4 cup of strawberries (sliced and hulled)
*1/8 cup of sherbet (raspberry)
*1/8 cup of whey protein powder
*1/2 of an orange (peeled and quartered)

Directions:

In a blender add 1/2 cup of cranberry juice, 1/2 cup of ice cubes, 1/4 cup of banana (chunked), 1/4 cup of strawberries (sliced and hulled), 1/8 cup of sherbet (raspberry), 1/8 cup of whey protein powder, and 1/2 of an orange (peeled and quartered) and blend until smooth. Pour in a glass and enjoy.

Fig Smoothie

A different flavor for smoothies, this one will be a favorite.

Makes 1 serving.

*10 figs
*1/2 cup of yogurt (vanilla Greek)
*1/2 cup of coconut milk
*1/2 cup of ice cubes
*1/4 cup of water
*1 tablespoon of flaxseed oil
*1 teaspoon of cinnamon (ground)

Directions:

In a blender add 10 figs, 1/2 cup of yogurt (vanilla Greek), 1/2 cup of coconut milk, 1/2 cup of ice cubes, 1/4 cup of water, 1 tablespoon of flaxseed oil, and 1 teaspoon of cinnamon (ground) and blend until smooth. Pour in a glass and enjoy.

Minty Melon-Umber Smoothie

This refreshing smoothie combines the delicious tastes of honeydew melon with a refreshing cucumber and fresh mint.

Makes 1 serving.

Ingredients:

*1/2 of a cumber (peeled, seeds removed and sliced)
*4 mint sprigs
*1 cup of ice (crushed)
*1 cup of honeydew melon (cubed)
*1 cup of passion fruit juice

Directions:

Prep: Remove the stems from the mint sprigs. Then in a blender add 1/2 of a cumber (peeled, seeds removed and sliced), 4 mint sprigs, 1 cup of ice (crushed), 1 cup of honeydew melon (cubed), and 1 cup of passion fruit juice and blend until smooth. Pour into a glass and enjoy.

Tangerine Smoothie

Not only will you enjoy the flavor of refreshing tangerine but also dragon fruit and lime with a touch of basil.

Makes 1 serving.

Ingredients:

*1 tangerine (peeled and quartered)
*2 basil leaves
*1/2 of a dragon fruit
*1/2 of a lime (juice only)
*1/2 cup of sparkling mineral water (cold)
*1/2 cup of ice (crushed)
*1 tablespoon of honey

Directions:

In a blender add 1 tangerine (peeled and quartered), 2 basil leaves, 1/2 of a dragon fruit, 1/2 of a lime (juice only), 1/2 cup of sparkling mineral water (cold), 1/2 cup of ice (crushed), and 1 tablespoon of honey and blend until smooth. Pour into a glass and enjoy.

Sweet Mango Smoothie

This is a delicious mango smoothie to satisfy the sweet tooth.

Makes 1 serving.

Ingredients:

*1/2 cup of yogurt
*1/4 cup of milk
*3/4 of a mango (peeled, seeds removed and chunked)
*1 teaspoon of honey
*dash of cardamom (ground)

Directions:

In a blender add 1/2 cup of yogurt, 1/4 cup of milk, 3/4 of a mango (peeled, seeds removed and chunked), and 1 teaspoon of honey and blend until smooth. Pour into a glass and place in the refrigerator for an hour. Sprinkle a dash of ground cardamom and serve.

Almond Banana Smoothie

When you combine almond butter with bananas, you get a delicious smoothie complete with a hint of cinnamon.

Makes 1 serving.

*1 banana (chunked and frozen)
*1 cup of milk
*1/2 tablespoon of almond butter
*1/2 teaspoon of vanilla extract
*dash of ground cinnamon

Directions:

In a blender, add 1 banana (chunked), 1 cup of milk, 1/2 tablespoon of almond butter, and 1/2 teaspoon of vanilla extract and blend until smooth. Pour into a glass and garnish with a dash of ground cinnamon. Enjoy.

Pumpkin Smoothie

Here is a delicious autumn smoothie that can be enjoyed year round because it calls for canned pumpkin puree.

Makes 1 serving.

Ingredients:

*1/2 cup of milk
*1/4 cup of pumpkin puree (frozen)
*1 tablespoon of honey
*1/2 teaspoon of cinnamon (ground)

Directions:

In a blender, add 1/2 cup of milk, 1/4 cup of frozen pumpkin puree, 1 tablespoon of honey, and 1/2 teaspoon of cinnamon (ground) and blend until smooth. Pour in a glass and enjoy.

Oatmeal and Fruit Smoothie

This is a stick to your ribs, satisfying smoothie.

Makes 1 serving.

Ingredients:

*1/2 cup of milk
*1/4 cup of oats (rolled)
*1/4 cup of bananas (chunked)
*7 strawberries (frozen)
*1/4 teaspoon of vanilla extract
*3/4 teaspoon of honey

Directions:

In a blender, add 1/2 cup of milk, 1/4 cup of oats (rolled), 1/4 cup of bananas (chunked), 7 strawberries (frozen), 1/4 teaspoon of vanilla extract, and 3/4 teaspoon of honey and blend until smooth. Pour into a glass and serve. Might want to serve with a spoon!

Pomegranate Smoothie

This is a refreshingly different fruit smoothie with pomegranates, mangoes and berries.

Makes 1 serving.

Ingredients:

*1/3 cup of milk
*1/4 cup of blueberries
*1/4 cup of raspberries
*1/4 cup of pomegranate juice
*1/4 cup of mango juice
*2 strawberries
*1 tablespoon of honey

Directions:

In a blender add 1/3 cup of milk, 1/4 cup of blueberries, 1/4 cup of raspberries, 1/4 cup of pomegranate juice, 1/4 cup of mango juice, 2 strawberries, and 1 tablespoon of honey and blend until smooth. Pour into a glass and enjoy. For a frosty smoothie freeze all the fruit first.

Melon Smoothie

This is a refreshing and thirst quenching smoothie.

Makes 1 serving.

Ingredients:

*1/2 cup of watermelon (no seeds, cubed)
*1/4 cup of honeydew melon (cubed)
*1/4 cup of milk
*2 tablespoons of ice cubes
*2 tablespoons of milk

Directions:

In a blender, add 1/2 cup of watermelon (no seeds, cubed), 1/4 cup of honeydew melon (cubed), 1/4 cup of milk, 2 tablespoons of ice cubes, and 2 tablespoons of milk and blend until smooth. Pour into a glass and enjoy.

Vegetable Smoothies (Also known as green smoothies)

Veggie Nut Smoothie

This is definitely a smoothie meant for lunch or supper.

Makes 1 serving.

Ingredients:

*3/4 cup of spinach
*1/2 cup of carrots (shredded)
*1/4 cup of beets (raw sliced)
*1/4 cup of milk
*1/4 cup of bananas (chunked)
*1/4 pear (no core, chopped)
*2 tablespoons of cottage cheese
*2 tablespoons of walnuts (chopped)
*2 tablespoons of almonds (chopped)
*1 tablespoon of yogurt (Greek)
*1 1/2 teaspoons of honey
*1/4 teaspoon of cinnamon (ground)

Directions:

In a blender add 3/4 cup of spinach, 1/2 cup of carrots (shredded), 1/4 cup of beets (raw sliced), 1/4 cup of milk, 1/4 cup of bananas (chunked), 1/4 pear (no core, chopped), 2 tablespoons of cottage cheese, 2 tablespoons of walnuts (chopped), 2 tablespoons of almonds (chopped), 1 tablespoon of yogurt (Greek), 1 1/2 teaspoons of honey, and 1/4 teaspoon of cinnamon (ground) and blend until smooth. Pour into a glass and enjoy.

Creamy Papaya Smoothie

A unique smoothie made with cream cheese.

Makes 1 serving.

Ingredients:

*1/3 cup papaya (peeled, seeded, chunked)
*1/3 cup of milk
*1/3 cup of ice
*2 1/4 tablespoons of yogurt (vanilla)
*2 teaspoons of honey
*2 teaspoons of sweetened condensed milk
*1 teaspoon of cream cheese

Directions:

In a blender add 1/3 cup papaya (peeled, seeded, chunked), 1/3 cup of milk, 1/3 cup of ice, 2 1/4 tablespoons of yogurt (vanilla), 2 teaspoons of honey, 2 teaspoons of sweetened condensed milk, and 1 teaspoon of cream cheese and blend until smooth. Pour in a glass and enjoy.

Strawberry Mud Smoothie

It is true, this smoothie looks like a glass of mud, but it tastes like sweet strawberry banana.

Makes 1 serving.

Ingredients:

*1/2 cup of spinach (frozen)
*1/2 cup of strawberries (frozen)
*1/4 cup of banana (chunked)
*2 tablespoons of ice
*1 1/2 teaspoon of honey

Directions:

In a blender, add 1/2 cup of spinach (frozen), 1/2 cup of strawberries (frozen), 1/4 cup of banana (chunked), 2 tablespoons of ice, and 1 1/2 teaspoon of honey and blend until smooth. Pour in a glass and enjoy. Really, it tastes better than it looks!

Zucchini Orange Smoothie

This beautiful light green colored smoothie tastes like delicious orange vanilla.

Makes 1 serving.

Ingredients:

*1/2 of a zucchini (cubed)
*3 ice cubes
*1/2 cup of orange juice
*1 tablespoon of honey
*1/4 teaspoon of vanilla extract

Directions:

In a blender, add 1/2 of a zucchini (cubed), 3 ice cubes, 1/2 cup of orange juice, 1 tablespoon of honey, and 1/4 teaspoon of vanilla extract and blend until smooth. Pour in a glass and enjoy.

Silly Sweet Zucchini Smoothie

It is silly sweet, because the only flavors you will taste in this smoothie are the bananas, cocoa and peanuts.

Makes 1 serving.

Ingredients:

*1/4 cup of zucchini (grated and frozen)
*1/4 cup of bananas (chunked)
*1/4 cup of half and half
*1/2 tablespoons of cocoa powder
*2 tablespoons of peanuts (finely chopped)
*1 tablespoon of honey

Directions:

In a blender add 1/4 cup of zucchini (grated and frozen), 1/4 cup of bananas (chunked), 1/4 cup of half and half, 1/2 tablespoons of cocoa powder, 2 tablespoons of peanuts (finely chopped), and 1 tablespoon of honey and blend until smooth. Pour into a glass and enjoy.

California Delight Smoothie

California is famous for their avocados and this smoothie is filled with them.

Makes 1 serving.

Ingredients:

*1/2 of an avocado (diced)
*1/4 cup of yogurt (vanilla)
*1/4 cup of milk
*1/8 cup of coconut cream
*4 ice cubes

Directions:

In a blender, add 1/2 of an avocado (diced), 1/4 cup of yogurt (vanilla), 1/4 cup of milk, 1/8 cup of coconut cream, and 4 ice cubes and blend until smooth. Pour in a glass and enjoy.

Pineapple Kiwi Smoothie

Not only will you taste pineapple and kiwi, but there is banana and the goodness of carrots in this smoothie.

Makes 1 serving.

Ingredients:

*1/2 cup of carrots (chopped)
*1/4 cup of banana (chopped)
*1/2 cup of apple (peeled, cored and chopped)
*1/2 cup of pineapple (chopped)
*1/2 cup of ice cubes
*1/4 cup of kiwi (peeled and chopped)

In a blender add: 1/2 cup of carrots (chopped), 1/4 cup of banana (chopped),1/2 cup of apple (peeled, cored and chopped), 1/2 cup of pineapple (chopped), 1/2 cup of ice cubes, and 1/4 cup of kiwi (peeled and chopped). Blend until smooth, pour into a glass, and enjoy.

Melon Cucumber Broccoli Smoothie

This smoothie turns into such a pretty shade of green, but tastes like fruit.

Makes 1 serving.

Ingredients:

*3/4 cup of honeydew melon (chunked)
*3/4 cup of ice cubes
*1/4 cup of grapes (green and seedless)
*1/4 cup of cucumber (no seeds and peeled)
*2 tablespoons of broccoli florets
*1/4 sprig of mint (fresh)

Directions:

In a blender add 3/4 cup of honeydew melon (chunked), 3/4 cup of ice cubes, 1/4 cup of grapes (green and seedless), 1/4 cup of cucumber (no seeds and peeled), 2 tablespoons of broccoli florets, and 1/4 sprig of mint (fresh) and blend until smooth. Pour in a glass and enjoy.

Truly Green Smoothie

Do not let the name fool you, it may be very green in color, but you will only taste the apples, pears, and cinnamon.

Makes 1 serving.

Ingredients:

*1/2 cup of apple juice
*1/2 cup of spinach
*1/3 cup of pears (chopped)
*1/3 cup of apples (chopped)
*1/2 teaspoon of cinnamon (ground)
*1/4 cup of ice

Directions:

Add the 1/2 cup of apple juice to a blender along with the 1/2 cup of spinach, 1/3 cup of chopped pears, 1/3 cup of chopped apples, 1/2 teaspoon of ground cinnamon, and the 1/4 cup of ice and blend until smooth. Pour in a glass and enjoy.

CocoCranNut Smoothie

This refreshing smoothie has way more than just coconut and cranberries, there are also avocados, cherries, blueberries and even basil. This is not your ordinary smoothie.

Makes 1 extra-large serving or 2 small servings.

Ingredients:

*1 cup of blueberries
*1 cup of yogurt (vanilla Greek)
*1/4 cup of cranberries (dried)
*1/4 cup of banana (chunked)
*1/2 avocado (pitted and chunked)
*10 cherries (pitted)
*5 cashews
*2 basil leaves (chopped)
*2 tablespoons of coconut flakes
*tablespoons of flax seeds (ground)
*1 teaspoon of chia seeds
*1 teaspoon of honey
*dash of cinnamon

Directions:

In the blender add 1 cup of blueberries, 1 cup of yogurt (vanilla Greek), 1/4 cup of cranberries (dried), 1/4 cup of banana (chunked), 1/2 avocado (pitted and chunked), 10 cherries (pitted), 5 cashews, 2 basil leaves (chopped), 2 tablespoons of coconut flakes, tablespoons of flax seeds (ground), 1 teaspoon of chia seeds, 1 teaspoon of honey, and a dash of cinnamon and blend until smooth. You may need to pulse at first to blend all the ingredients. Pour into a large glass or two small glasses and enjoy.

Gingered Veggie Fruit Smoothie

This smoothie is not only delicious but serves as a great supper substitute or for lunch.

Makes 1 serving.

Ingredients:

*2 cups of water (cold)
*1 avocado (peeled, pitted and chopped)
*1 apple (core removed and chopped)
*1 carrot (chunks)
*1 lemon (peeled and quartered)
*1 kale leaf
*1 piece of ginger root (1 inch)
*1/2 cup of parsley (fresh)
*1 tablespoon of flax seeds
*2 ice cubes

Directions:

First, pour the 2 cups of cold water into the blender and add the peeled, pitted and chopped avocado, cored and chopped apple, chunked carrot, peeled and quartered lemon, the kale leaf (rip it apart), the 1 inch ginger root (chopped), 1/2 cup of fresh parsley, tablespoon of flax seeds and blend until it reaches desired texture. Pour in a glass and enjoy.

Rhubarb Fruit Smoothie

Even though rhubarb is a vegetable, it is often used in desserts because of its sweet flavor.

Makes 1 serving.

Ingredients:

*1/2 cup of rhubarb (chopped and frozen)
*1/2 cup of cranberry juice
*1/4 cup of yogurt (vanilla)
*1/4 cup of banana (chunks)
*1 teaspoon of honey

Directions:

Add the 1/2 cup of chopped, frozen rhubarb, 1/2 cup of cranberry juice, 1/4 cup of vanilla yogurt, 1/4 cup of banana chunks and the teaspoon of honey into a blender and blend until it reaches desired consistency. Pour into a glass and enjoy.

Banana Chocolate Mint Green Smoothie

A delightful twist with a smoothie with the addition of chocolate and mint with the hidden goodness of spinach.

Makes 1 serving.

Ingredients:

*1/2 cup of spinach leaves
*1/4 cup of coconut milk (chilled)
*1/4 cup of banana (chopped frozen)
*1/8 cup of cocoa powder (unsweetened)
*5 mint leaves (fresh chopped)
*1/2 gram of stevia powder
*1/2 teaspoon of peppermint extract
*ice
*water

Directions:

In a blender add the 1/2 cup of spinach leaves, 1/4 cup of chilled coconut milk, 1/8 cup of unsweetened cocoa powder, 5 fresh chopped mint leaves, 1/2 gram of stevia powder, 1/2 teaspoon of peppermint extract. Blend until well mixed. Add the 1/4 cup of chopped frozen banana and blend. Add ice and or water and blend until desired consistency. Pour into a glass and enjoy.

Spicy Tomato Smoothie

Enjoy this savory vegetable infused smoothie.

Makes 1 serving.

Ingredients:

*1 cup of tomatoes (chopped)
*1 cup of ice
*1/4 cup of tomato juice
*1/4 cup of carrots (chopped)
*1/8 cup of celery (chopped)
*1/8 cup of apple juice
*dash of hot sauce

Directions:

In a blender, add the 1/4 cup of chopped carrots and 1/8 cup of chopped celery with the 1/8 cup of apple juice and blend until vegetables are pureed. Add the cup of chopped tomatoes, cup of ice and the 1/4 cup of tomato juice and blend along with the dash of hot sauce. Blend until it reaches desired consistency. Pour into glass and enjoy.

Broccoli Smoothie

Broccoli is one of the super foods therefore this is one healthy and tasty smoothie.

Makes 1 serving.

Ingredients:

*4 broccoli florets
*2 oranges (peeled)
*1 carrot (chopped)
*1 apple (cored and chopped)
*2 cups of spinach
*orange juice as needed

Directions:

First, you may want to juice the carrot and apple, if not, just chop them up into small chunks. Add the 4 broccoli florets, 2 oranges (quartered), chopped or juiced carrot and apple, 2 cups of spinach (loosely chopped) into a blender. Drizzle some orange juice and blend until it reaches desired consistency. Add more orange juice if needed. Pour into a glass and enjoy.

Orange Carrot Cantaloupe Smoothie

This is a refreshing smoothie with carrots, but all you taste is the delicious cantaloupe.

Makes 1 serving.

Ingredients:

*1 cup of cantaloupe (diced and ripe)
*1/2 cup of carrot juice
*1/2 cup of frozen yogurt (vanilla)
*1 tablespoon of orange juice (straight from the frozen concentrate can)

Directions:

Add the 1 cup of diced ripe cantaloupe, 1/2 cup of carrot juice, 1/2 cup of frozen vanilla yogurt and tablespoon of frozen orange juice concentrate to the blender and blend until smooth. Pour into glass and enjoy.

Avocado Maple Smoothie

This smoothie gives energy because it is a well-balanced drink.

Makes 1 serving.

Ingredients:

*1 avocado (peeled, pitted, cubed)
*1 cup of whey protein powder (vanilla)
*1/4 cup of ice
*1/4 cup of milk
*1/8 cup of sweetened condensed milk
*1/8 cup of maple syrup

Directions:

Add the peeled, pitted and cubed avocado to a blender along with the cup of vanilla whey protein powder, 1/4 cup of ice, 1/4 cup of milk, 1/8 cup of sweetened condensed milk and 1/8 cup of maple syrup. Blend until smooth and pour into glass to serve.

Spicy Vegetable Smoothie

This hot and savory smoothie is definitely not your typical breakfast smoothie; this is more for lunch or supper.

Makes 1 serving.

Ingredients:

*4 cups of celery (chopped)
*2 cups of tomatoes (chopped)
*2 red bell peppers (chopped)
*1 zucchini
*1/4 cup of onions (sliced)
*1/4 cup of avocado (chunked)
*1 tablespoon of chili powder
*1 teaspoon of flax seeds
*1/2 teaspoon of dulse flakes
*dash of cayenne pepper
*1 celery stalk

Directions:

First, add the 2 cups of chopped tomatoes in a blender and puree. Next, add the 2 chopped red bell peppers and the chopped zucchini and blend. Next, add the 4 cups of chopped celery, 1/4 cup of sliced onions, 1/4 cup of chunked avocado, tablespoon of chili powder, teaspoon of flax seeds, 1/2 teaspoon of dulse flakes and a dash of cayenne pepper. Pour into a tall glass, garnish with the stalk of celery, and enjoy.

Kale Smoothie

Here is a vegetable smoothie that will taste like cool grapes.

Makes 1 serving.

Ingredients:

*1 cup of grapes (green seedless)
*1 cup of kale
*1/2 cup of ice cubes

Directions:

Add the cups of green seedless grapes and kale in the blender along with the 1/2 cup of ice cubes. Blend until smooth, pour in a glass and enjoy.

Vanilla Yam Smoothie

Yams are naturally sweet and this makes this vegetable smoothie even sweeter.

Makes 1 serving.

Ingredients:

*1/4 of a yam (cooked)
*1/3 cup of yogurt (vanilla)
*1/4 cup of ice (crushed)
*1/4 cup of banana (chunked)
*1/8 cup of milk
*drizzle of honey (to taste)

Directions:

In a blender add 1/4 of a yam (cooked), 1/3 cup of yogurt (vanilla), 1/4 cup of ice (crushed), 1/4 cup of banana (chunked), 1/8 cup of milk, and then a drizzle of honey (to taste) and blend until smooth. Pour in a glass and enjoy.

Sweet Potato Banana Smoothie

Another naturally sweet vegetable smoothie this time using sweet potato.

Makes 1 serving.

Ingredients:

*1 cup of milk
*1/2 of a sweet potato (baked)
*1/4 cup of banana (chunked)
*1/8 teaspoon of cinnamon (ground)

Directions:

Prep: After baking the sweet potato, place in refrigerator for several hours or overnight to completely cool. Remove peel.

In a blender, add 1 cup of milk, 1/2 of a sweet potato (baked, peeled and cooled), 1/4 cup of banana (chunked), and 1/8 teaspoon of cinnamon (ground) and blend until smooth. Pour in a glass and enjoy.

Banana Kale Orange Smoothie

All you taste is the banana and orange in this delicious vegetable smoothie.

Makes 1 serving.

Ingredients:

*1 orange (peeled and quartered)
*1 kale leaf (torn into pieces)
*1/2 cup of water (cold)
*1 cup of bananas (chunked)

Directions:

First, add the orange in the blender and blend. Next, add the 1/2 cup of cold water and the kale leaf pieces and blend. Last, add the cup of banana chunks and blend until smooth. Smoothie will be thick. Pour in a glass and drink or spoon eat.

Eat Your Vegetables Smoothie

This smoothie has spinach and carrots, but you will taste the apples, orange, bananas and strawberries!
Makes 1 serving.

Ingredients:

*1/2 cup of spinach
*1/4 cup of bananas (chunked)
*1/4 cup of carrots (finely chopped)
*1/4 cup of orange juice
*1/4 cup of strawberries
*1/4 cup of ice
*half an apple (peeled, cored and chopped)

Directions:

In a blender add 1/2 cup of spinach, 1/4 cup of bananas (chunked), 1/4 cup of carrots (finely chopped), 1/4 cup of orange juice, 1/4 cup of strawberries, 1/4 cup of ice, and half an apple (peeled, cored and chopped) and blend until smooth. Pour in a glass and enjoy.

Tofu Smoothies

Chocolate Tofu Smoothie

A healthy smoothie with the favored flavor of chocolate combined with the healthy protein of tofu.

Makes 1 serving.

Ingredients:

*1/2 cup of milk
*1/4 cup of tofu (silken, chunked)
*1/4 cup of banana (chunks)
*1/3 tablespoon of honey
*2/3 tablespoon of chocolate drink mix
*1/8 tablespoon of wheat germ

Directions:

In a blender, add the 1/2 cup of milk, 1/4 cup of tofu (silken, chunked), 1/4 cup of banana (chunks), 1/3 tablespoon of honey, 2/3 tablespoon of chocolate drink mix, and 1/8 tablespoon of wheat germ and blend until smooth. Pour in a glass and enjoy.

Banana Berry Tofu Smoothie

The delicious combination of strawberries, blueberries and banana combined with protein rich tofu makes this a nutritious smoothie.

Makes 1 serving.

Ingredients:

*1/2 cup of yogurt (vanilla)
*1/2 cup of milk
*1/2 cup of strawberries
*1/3 cup of blueberries
*1/4 cup of banana
*1 1/2 inch cube of tofu (soft)

Directions:

Add the 1/2 cup of vanilla yogurt to a blender along with the 1/2 cup of milk, 1/4 cup of banana and the 1 1/2 inch cube of soft tofu, and blend until smooth. Add the 1/2 cup of strawberries and 1/3 cup of blueberries and blend again. Pour into a glass and enjoy.

Apple Strawberry Banana Smoothie

Protein rich smoothie with the flavor of apples, strawberries, and bananas.

Makes 1 serving.

Ingredients:

*1/2 cup of strawberries
*1/4 cup of apple juice
*1/4 cup of yogurt (frozen vanilla)
*1/4 cup of tofu (soft)
*1/4 cup of banana (chunked)
*1/4 cup of ice cubes
*1/2 tablespoon of honey
*1 strawberry (sliced)

In a blender add the 1/2 cup of strawberries, 1/4 cup of apple juice, 1/4 cup of frozen vanilla yogurt, 1/4 cup of soft tofu, 1/4 cup of chunked banana, 1/2 tablespoon of honey and blend until smooth. Add the 1/4 cup of ice cubes and blend until smooth. Pour into a glass, garnish with the sliced strawberries, and enjoy.

Apple Peach Banana Smoothie

Protein rich smoothie with the flavor of apples, peaches, and bananas.

Makes 1 serving.

Ingredients:

*1/2 cup of peaches (chunked)
*1/4 cup of apple juice
*1/4 cup of peach sorbet
*1/4 cup of tofu (soft)
*1/4 cup of banana (chunked)
*1/4 cup of ice cubes
*1/2 tablespoon of honey
*1 peach slice

In a blender add the 1/2 cup of strawberries, 1/4 cup of apple juice, 1/4 cup of peach sorbet, 1/4 cup of soft tofu, 1/4 cup of chunked banana, 1/2 tablespoon of honey and blend until smooth. Add the 1/4 cup of ice cubes and blend until smooth. Pour into a glass, garnish with the sliced peach, and enjoy.

Banana Raspberry Tofu Smoothie

Classic tofu makes a smoothie a complete meal replacement.

Makes 1 serving.

Ingredients:

*1/4 cup of tofu (silken)
*1/4 cup of milk
*1/4 cup of banana (chunked
*1/4 cup of raspberries
**2 tablespoons of orange juice (from frozen concentrate can)

Directions:

In a blender, add 1/4 cup of tofu (silken), 1/4 cup of milk, 1/4 cup of banana (chunked), 1/4 cup of raspberries, and 2 tablespoons of orange juice (from frozen concentrate can) and blend until smooth. Pour into a glass and enjoy.

5 Day Sample Menu

The smoothie diet is a diet in which these smoothie recipes are meant to replace an entire meal. This helps in two ways, first to facilitate weight loss, and second to reduce hunger. If you are counting calories, you can adjust the ingredients to accommodate more or less caloric intake. For example, use low fat or skim milk instead of 2% or whole milk. Use low fat yogurt, or light soymilk. Adjust according to your dieting needs.

Most of the smoothies in this book have protein in the form of a dairy product, soy, tofu, or even added protein powder. A few do not and those should be used as snacks or desserts only and not a full meal replacement. When preparing smoothies, most are best consumed immediately. A few may last a day or two if stored in the refrigerator, especially those with no frozen ingredients. Fruit juice smoothies may last several days whereas dairy foods will make them less able to last longer than a day or two.

If you follow the smoothie diet, eating all the meals including the snacks, the hunger should stay away. If you skip any of the suggested meals, you will become hungry and a smoothie alone may not satisfy you. The goal is to make the stomach think it is full at all times. Smoothies are a healthy way to receive the vitamins and minerals contains in fruits and vegetables. For many people it is a very easy diet to follow and stick with and experience successful weight loss.

Day One

Breakfast
Peanut Banana Berry Smoothie

Mid-Morning Snack
An apple

Lunch
Apple Strawberry Banana Smoothie

Mid-Afternoon Snack
Grapefruit half

Supper
Avocado Maple Smoothie

Day Two

Breakfast
Fruit Spread Smoothie

Mid-Morning Snack
An orange

Lunch
Kale Smoothie

Mid-Afternoon Snack
Small bunch of grapes

Supper
A whole food plate of vegetables and one lean serving of meat

Day Three

Breakfast
Creamy Strawberry Smoothie

Mid-Morning Snack
Glass of all-natural fruit punch

Lunch
Apple Peach Banana Smoothie

Mid-Afternoon Snack
Sliced Kiwi

Supper
Orange Carrot Cantaloupe Smoothie

Day Four

Breakfast
Refreshing Smoothie

Mid-Morning Snack
A small bunch of grapes

Lunch
Spicy Vegetable Smoothie

Mid-Afternoon Snack
An apple

Supper
A whole food plate of vegetables and one lean serving of meat

Day Five

Breakfast
Peachy Banana Berry Smoothie

Mid-Morning Snack
A grapefruit half

Lunch
Banana Berry Tofu Smoothie

Mid-Afternoon Snack
All-natural fruit punch

Supper
Broccoli Smoothie

This sample menu has a choice of a whole foods supper every other day. If you are too hungry and need more solid food, make every night a whole food supper. Or the opposite, if you can handle all smoothies all day, then go ahead and do that. This diet will help to lose weight and doing an all smoothie all day will help it to happen faster.

Section 2: Smoothie Diet

What is a smoothie? What makes it so much different from any other type of drink on the market? The biggest difference of course is that the smoothie is a blended drink, containing a number of different ingredients. While some smoothies are designed for taste, others are designed for health. Then again, you always have the in-between ground wherein you can have both taste AND health benefits!

Before you get started with your smoothing making adventure, it would be within your best interest to make sure you have the right tools on hand. The most common items you are going to need, and find in common with all of the recipes in this book, is a blender. While most smoothies can be made with any blender, you will need to make sure you have a particularly high end one if you are going to be making vegetable smoothies. It can be a bit difficult to blend broccoli and carrots properly, and as you know, even a juicer might not get it right the first ten times.

A smoothie is comprised of a few different ingredients, and once you look over the recipes named in this book, you might even try experimenting with a few of your own. The most important thing to remember however, is that while smoothies taste great, they are intended to sustain your health and even get you to a better place in your life. That being said, make sure you are using healthy ingredients, and most importantly, make sure you are using the right smoothie for the right occasion. Some are suitable for breakfast, some are great for lunches, and others are perfect for that energy boost you need first thing in the morning. Then again, some smoothies are better for the all-important liver purge.

Common Smoothie Ingredients:

Chocolate
Peanut Butter
Fruit
Frozen Fruit
Crushed Ice
Honey
Syrup
Milk
Yogurt
Soy Milk
Whey Powder
Green Tea

Though these are some of the most common ingredients, we don't recommend that you add them all at once. Instead, we are going to provide you a few great recipes in the following categories:

Fruit smoothies

Green Smoothies

Breakfast Smoothies

Energy Smoothies

Before we get into the different smoothie recipes, let's talk a bit about the detox diet along with the function of the liver. Before you attempt to perform a liver detox however, it would be within your best interest to get to know the liver and understand just why it needs detox from time to time.

Liver Detox and You

Every system, whether organic or mechanical will need some type of filter. In the human body, the liver serves as the primary filter, and it is virtually impossible to maintain good health without it. The problem however is that we tend to abuse our 'filter' over time, and it will lead to some type of illness. If you want to stop this illness from occurring, there are a few things you need to do. First of all you need to make sure you remove all the excess fat from the liver. In addition to that, bile needs to flow free, and toxic waste must be filtered out. If possible, gallstones should be dissolved and passed while regenerating damaged cells.

Many people consider the liver to be the most important organ in the body, but when it comes to healthcare it is ironically forgotten. With 200 separate identified functions, the liver is vital for regulating and breaking down different substances inside the body. These functions include, but are not limited to the following:

Fat Storage Regulation
Blood Cleansing
Discharge of Waste
Energy Production

Hormone Balance
Tissue Regeneration(Self)
Storage of Vitamins and Minerals
Metabolize Alcohol
Manufacture New Proteins
Produce Immune Factors
Remove Bacteria from Blood Stream
Manage Chemicals

While the average person might not give the liver a second thought, there are many in the medical profession who are of the opinion that a great number of diseases can actually be prevented completely if the liver is in working order. An unhealthy liver will be like a gateway to all sort of disease and should be corrected as quickly as possible.

Harm can come to the liver in a number of different ways. One such event might involve an excess of protein in the diet, while you might also find that simple carbohydrates do their share of harm. The more fat you have stored in the liver, the harder it is for the liver to actually function. This is something for you to think about the next time you choose to eat an entire plate of fried chicken.

Overeating is another issue and serious temptation that

we all face. Not only is overeating hard on the figure, it also provides too much enzyme deficient food and stresses the liver. One thing that pharmaceutical companies likely won't tell you is that drug residue is typically left in the body after medications have been taken. This of course is second only to the inflammation caused by alcohol and other chemicals. The icing on the cake is a lack of exercise, which forces the liver to do elimination work typically performed by the skin and lungs.

Some of the most common problems in the liver can include digestive problems, constipation, low energy output, hay fever, diabetes, obesity, and even hypertension. As you can see, these are issues that you really want to avoid! But what do you do about it? The liver, fortunately, is an organ that is more than capable of repairing itself if you give it a chance. In spite of this, you need to do your best to keep healthy, and ensure that your liver is capable of functioning normally.

How do you know what sort of diet to use? As a rule, you should try to diet depending on the severity of the illness you are facing. In other words, the sicker you are, the more you need to clean up your diet. In any case, it is strongly recommended that you do a liver cleanse/detox at least three to four times per year. The smoothies listed in this ebook should give you some idea and perhaps even help you to start a healthier life.

Smoothies And Weight Loss

In the United States of America obesity is rampant -- this is an indisputable fact. With regulations being passed on food servings and the weight of the average school child skyrocketing, the need for action has never been more dire. Obesity can lead to heart disease among other rather nasty conditions, and with that being the case, many are turning to more alternative diets including the Atkins and Mediterranean. The problems with these diets have been kindly pointed out by nutritionists for years, though none so much as the Atkins diet. With the Atkins diet you will completely forego the inclusion of carbohydrates within your diet, and while this will eventually cause you to lose weight, you will find that it can have other side effects as well. As a matter of fact, many people have actually died using the Atkins diet! That being said, it is important to find a diet that will meet your needs without causing you to drop dead at work or at school. This is where the Smoothie Diet will come into play.

Why would you be able to lose more weight with smoothies than other diets? Many of them taste downright outstanding, and as you know, you can't lose weight with something that tastes good. The truth however is that a smoothie will give you all of the necessary nutrients in a single glass without the unnecessary calories. As you learn more about smoothies and study the ingredients you will find that you can build a great combination that balances protein, healthy fats, vitamins, nutrients, and complex carbohydrates.

Yes, smoothies can be designed to help you lose weight, but you may also find it necessary to develop one that boost your metabolic rate. This will of course involve providing you with more energy, and filling you up. Gaining energy in this manner will save you from needing to head to the store and grab one of those Five Hour Energy drinks. There is nothing quite like doing it naturally, and let's face it, Mother Nature has all the ingredients we require, and she is more than willing to cater to our needs if we just listen.

Benefits of Soy Milk

Throughout this e-Book you may see us refer to Soy Milk or Almond Milk quite a bit. There is a reason for this! Soy milk is much healthier than regular milk, being naturally high in essential fatty acids, proteins, fiber, vitamins, and of course, minerals. These are the nutrients your body needs to function at maximum capacity, though you might be wondering exactly what Soy Milk can do for you in the long run.

The first thing that people will notice (if they are paying attention) is the improvement of their lipid profile. Unlike dairy milk, soy milk does not feature the same saturated fat or cholesterol. Soy milk is typically unsaturated, features no cholesterol, and is actually capable of inhibiting the transport of cholesterol into your bloodstream using the monounsaturated and polyunsaturated fatty acids. Regular intake of soy can actually lower triglycerides and LDL, or low density lipoproteins. If you have a history of heart disease in your family, soy milk might be the answer for you. In any case, it is always the answer when it comes to a proper smoothie weight loss diet.

What about blood vessel integrity? This is just as vital when it comes to basic survival, and it is another reason that we tend to include soy milk so often in our recipes. Soy contains omega-3 and omega-6 fatty acids along with phyto-antioxidants that will serve to protect your blood vessels from hemorrhage. These will also protect your lining cells from free radical attacks as well as cholesterol deposits. This is yet another reason why smoothies will help you lose weight AND keep your body in top shape.

Finally we have weight loss. That's why we're here, right? Though most people don't realize it, milk actually contains sugar by itself. Cow's milk contains 12 grams of sugar per cup, though soy milk only contains 7 grams per cup. Because soy milk only has 80 calories, it is the equivalent of skim milk. Through drinking soy milk you will gain extra fiber, and ultimately feel full for a longer period of time.

In a Nutshell:

Less Sugar than Cow Milk
Supports Blood Vessel Integrity
No Cholesterol
Inhibits Transport of Cholesterol to Bloodstream
Lowers Triglycerides and LDL
Encourages Weight Loss

In the end soy milk might be a bit more expensive than regular milk, but it will help you to feel fuller for longer, and will eventually drive your food costs down. In addition to that you will feel much healthier in the coming weeks.

Part 1: Fruit Smoothies

Fruit smoothies are not necessarily a health smoothie, though they do help individuals to lose weight. These smoothies do a great job of creating a meal replacement diet, ultimately giving you a tasty treat whenever you need one! Fruit smoothies are great for breakfast or for a quick snack at any point during the day. The best part is the way they fill you up. Rather than empty calories, fruit smoothies provide all the nutrients you require to keep you full and keep your hand out of the cookie jar. Each fruit smoothie will obviously consist of a base, and many people choose to use a banana. Others will opt for various flavors of yogurt, and in the end, it is totally up to you. You have so many different choices for bases and flavors, so go over the following recipes and see which suits you best for your day to day meal replacement!

Recipe #1. The Basic Fruit Smoothie:

What we have here is the basic fruit smoothie containing all of the ingredients you need to embark on your own sensational adventure in taste. From strawberries to chunked banana, you have all the essential fruits and more if you feel like experimenting!

Items Needed:

Blender or Smoothie Maker
Glasses

Ingredients:

1 Quart Hulled Strawberries
1 Chunked Banana
2 Peaches Pitted and Chunked
2 Cups of Ice (Small Chunks)
1 Cup of Orange, Peach, or Mango Juice

Preparation Instructions:

Place all of the fruit in a large blender, use the high setting until fruit is pureed. Once this is accomplished, add in your choice of orange, peach, or mango juice and continue blending until you achieve the consistency you want. Once completed, you may pour into glasses garnish with a slice of fruit and serve.

Note: Because this is the basic smoothie, you may feel free to try different ingredient combinations for different taste experiences.

Recipe #2: The Frozen Banana Smoothie

Though this is a smoothie of the frozen banana variety, banana will not be used as the base. Instead, low-fat Vanilla Yogurt will be used along with an amount of orange juice. All of the ingredients are fairly soft, meaning you can use a basic blender rather than a smoothie maker or juicer. This is one of the easiest smoothies to make so long as you have all of the ingredients on hand or can get to them easily.

Items Needed:

Blender or Smoothie Maker
Glasses

Ingredients:

1 Cup of Sliced Strawberries
1 6 oz cup of Low-fat Vanilla Yogurt
2 Frozen Bananas
2/3 Cup of Pulp-Free Orange Juice

Preparation Instructions:

Place the fruit ingredients into the blender on high and blend until fruit is pureed. Add yogurt pulsing it just enough to start the mixing process. Next pour in the juice and blend on medium until you reach the desired thickness. Pour into your glasses and serve.

Recipe #3: The Banana Berry Colada

Though you might not live near a beach, there is no reason you shouldn't be able to enjoy a tropical drink here and there – even if you're on a diet. This recipe brings the tropical island feel to you, and gives you the taste you crave without the alcoholic aftertaste.

Items Needed:

Blender or Smoothie Maker
Glasses

Ingredients:

3 Cups of Small Cubed Ice
1/2 Cup of Frozen Strawberries
1 Cup Pina Colada Mix
2 Whole Frozen Bananas
1/2 Cup of Yogurt

Preparation Instructions:

Layer all the ingredients in your blender and blend on high for about 80 to 90 seconds. Serve immediately.

Note: If you cannot find strawberries(they occasionally

go out of season) you can use strawberry syrup as a substitute.

Recipe #4: The Basic Grape Smoothie

For this recipe most people will actually recommend that you use red grapes, though to be perfectly honest you can use anything you want. Keep in mind that the ingredients mentioned make for a great smoothie, but you can replace the skim milk with regular milk, or the plain yogurt with low fat yogurt. Feel free to experiment and come up with the perfect combination for your needs.

Items Needed:

Blender or Smoothie Maker
Glasses

Ingredients:

2 Cups of Seedless Grapes of any color
1 Cup of Skim Milk
2 Tablespoons of Sugar
1 Cup of Plain Yogurt

Preparation Instructions:

Place grapes and sugar into the blender on medium and mix thoroughly. Add in the yogurt and blend for another

10 seconds on medium. Pour in the milk and blend on high. Proceed with this until the mixture is perfectly smooth.

Note: Though you are free to use any type of grape for this smoothie, it is recommended that you purchase a bushel of seedless grapes to avoid not having enough for everyone.

Recipe #5: Raspberry-Orange Smoothie

Orange is in fashion with this smoothie, but before you embark on this journey of taste, make sure you are actually using pulp free orange juice. In addition to that, you should of course make sure you are using ice cubes rather than chipped ice or straight water. The last thing you want to do is water down a tasty smoothie!

Items Needed:

Blender or Smoothie Maker
Glasses

Ingredients:

1 Cup Pulp Free Orange Juice
1 Cup of Raspberries
1/2 Cup of Plain Yogurt
2 Cup Sugar
1 Cup of Small Cube Ice
1 Sprig of Mint for garnish

Preparation Instructions:

Place your orange juice, raspberries, and sugar into your blender, mix on medium for 60 seconds. Add in the yogurt and blend for another 30 seconds. Toss in your ice and blend on high until you have the thickness desired. Pour into your glasses, garnish with a sprig of mint and serve.

Recipe #6: Kiwi-Apple Smoothie

If you're ready for something tasty then you've come to the right place. This mixture of fruits and vegetables might as well be a taste of heaven, and the best part is you can choose which leafy greens you want to include in your new concoction. Then again, you are free to experiment and remove the greens entirely! Remember – the smoothie is your oyster!

Items Needed:

Blender or Smoothie Maker
Glasses

Ingredients:

2 Kiwi Fruit Peeled
2 Apples Peeled and Cored
2 Cups Leafy Greens
1 Full Size Carrot
1/2 Cup of Water

Preparation Instructions:

Place the carrots and apples into the blender, pulse until small enough pieces to place the blender on high for another 60 seconds. Put in the leafy greens and water, blend on high for 30 seconds. Then add in the kiwis. Blend again on high until your desired thickness. Garnish with a slice of kiwi fruit if desired and serve.

Note: The leafy green may be lettuce or spinach. Baby spinach is recommended.

Recipe #7: Apple-Lemon Smoothie

Are you ready to try something sweet and sour? You've come to the right page! For this one all you need are a few ingredients and a bit of imagination. It's time to give your taste buds an experience that they will never forget, at least until you drink your next cup of hot coffee.

Items Needed:

Blender or Smoothie Maker
Glasses

Ingredients:

2 Apples (Any variety)
1 Full Sized Carrot
1/2 Cup of Water
2 Cups of Leafy Greens

Preparation Instructions:

Clean and peel your carrot, leaving one peel for garnish. Then slice the remaining it into small chunks. Core and cube your apples. Toss your carrots it into the blender. Pulse a few times and then add in the apples and water.

Keep pulsing until partially smooth. Add in your leafy greens, and put the blender on high until the desired consistency is reached. Pour into a glass and garnish with a strip of carrot on top.

Note: The leafy green may be lettuce or spinach. Baby spinach is recommended. It is also important to remember that apple skin must be left intact. While the apple should be ripe, it should not be brown on the interior or close to rotten. The skin of the apple contains plenty of nutrients and will help contribute to a healthy diet. That being said, choose your apples carefully and make sure you are using the same two apples in your smoothie. For example if you use a Gala apple, use two Galas, or if you use a Red Delicious, make sure the other is Red Delicious as well. The result will be a delicious meal replacement snack!

Recipe #8: Pear-Nut Smoothie

This recipe, unlike some of the others we have mentioned previously actually uses water as a base rather than yogurt or banana, even though banana is used as a core ingredient in this recipe. Keep in mind that you are using a peeled, frozen banana in this recipe, so it might be a good idea to invest in a high end blender or a smoothie maker not only to ensure that there is no damage to the device, but also to ensure that you achieve a perfect mixture. In addition to that, it may be helpful to acquire a glass blender container as these tend to be tougher.

Items Needed:

Blender or Smoothie Maker
Glasses

Ingredients:

1 Frozen and Peeled Banana
1/4 Cup Raw nuts
2 pears cored
1/2 Cup of Water
12 Ice Cubes

Preparation Instructions:

Pour water into your blender. Start layering your ingredients with the nuts on bottom, pears and ice in the middle and the bananas on top. Blend on low speed for 20 seconds. Increase to high speed until drink becomes smooth.

Recipe #9: Nutty Creamy Apple Smoothie

If you're not allergic to nuts then you might find this smoothie agreeable to your pallet. If you are, then you can always remove the nuts. Keep in mind that this recipe uses both water and yogurt as the base, making it a rather unique concoction. If you find that you do not like the consistency, you are always free to change it and experiment with different mixtures.

Items Needed:

Blender or Smoothie Maker
Glasses

Ingredients:

1 Banana, Peeled/Frozen
1/4 Cup Raw nuts
2 apples cored
1/2 Cup of Water
6 oz Plain Yogurt
12 Ice Cubes

Preparation Instructions:

Pour water into blender, layer the ingredients with the

nuts on the bottom, apples and ice in the middle and the banana and yogurt on top. Blend on low speed for 20 seconds. Increase to high speed until drink becomes smooth.

Recipe #10: Apple-Blueberry Smoothie

Apple and Blueberry are not typically seen together outside of a pancake or waffle setting, but they make a great smoothie along with avocado and leafy greens. You would do well to give this smoothie a try and augment your diet!

Items Needed:

Blender or Smoothie Maker
Glasses

Ingredients:

1 Cup of Blueberries
1 Apple
2 Cups of Leafy Greens
¼ Cup of Avocado
½ Cup of Water

Preparation Instructions:

Peel and remove the pit on the avocado then remove the core on the apple and cube both fruits. Pour the water into the blender, then toss in your apple. Pulse a few times to help break it down then add in the rest of your ingredients. Blend on medium for 30 seconds, then on high until you reach the desired consistency. Pour into your glass and top with one whole blueberry then serve.

Recipe #11: Cherry Apple Smoothie

Cherries and apples are always going to be popular. After all, they taste pretty great, don't they? This smoothie combines the two along with leafy greens, though as always, you may feel free to remove the leafy greens and make it exclusively fruit.

Items Needed:

Blender or Smoothie Maker
Glasses

Ingredients:

1 Cup cherries
1 Whole apple
2 Cups of fresh Leafy Green
½ Cup of Pure Water

Preparation Instructions:

Remove the stems and seeds from the cherries. Then core and cube your apple. In your blender add in your water and apple. Pulse these two items together for 30 seconds. Next add in the rest of your ingredients and blend on high until the smoothie is of the desired thickness. Pour into a glass and serve.

Recipe #12: CranBananaSmoothie

Though this smoothie might be filled with leafy greens, it is still not considered a green smoothie. By adding ½ cup of cranberries and a banana, we are creating what might be one of the healthiest and tastiest smoothies out there. That being said, you will most certainly want to put this one to the test as soon as you get the chance. Be warned that this DOES use water as a base, and therefore might not be quite as thick as most would prefer.

Items Needed:

Blender or Smoothie Maker
Glasses

Ingredients:

1/2 cup cranberries
1 Banana
2 cups fresh Leafy Greens
1 stalk of organic celery
3 Dates for Sweetening Purposes
4-6 Ounces of Water

Preparation Instructions:

Place the celery and water into your blender pulse 10 times to start breaking it down. Then add in the leafy greens, pulsing another 10 times. Toss in all of the fruit and blend on medium until desired consistency is achieved. Pour into your glass and enjoy.

Recipe #13: Plum-Apple-LemonSmoothie

This is another recipe that uses water as a base, but there is nothing quite like a good plum. These fruits have an entirely different taste, and make an outstanding addition to any smoothie. Combined with lemon juice and apple, you know your taste buds are in for the ultimate treat.

Items Needed:

Blender or Smoothie Maker
Glasses

Ingredients:

1 Plum Deseeded
1 Apple Cored
½ Lemon juiced
2 Cups of fresh Baby Spinach
1 Medium Carrot, Chopped
1/2 cup water

Preparation Instructions:

Place the water and chopped carrot into the blender use pulse a few times to help to break down the carrot. Add in the apple and pulse another 10 times. Layer in the last of the ingredients and starting on low speed work your way up to high until smooth. Pour into a glass and enjoy.

Recipe #14: Plum-Banana Smoothie

Because this recipe does not actually call for a frozen banana, you can use one at room temperature, and you will be able to use a blender rather than a smoothie maker. As always, try to ensure that all of the fruit is deseeded and preferably ripened.

Items Needed:

Blender or Smoothie Maker
Glasses

Ingredients:

2 plums, deseeded
1 banana, peeled
2 cups fresh baby spinach (or other leafy green)
½ vine ripe tomato
1/2 – 1 cup water

Preparation Instructions:

Pour the water into the blender with the plumbs and tomato. Blend on the low setting for 30 seconds. Then add in the leafy greens and banana blending on high until well blended and you reach the thickness desired.

Recipe #15: Kiwi-Banana Smoothie

This is yet another recipe that makes use of bananas, though we also have kiwis in the mixture. It is important to ensure you have enough kiwis if you choose to use the baby variant. Ideally you would obtain full grown kiwis, but sometimes the store simply does not have them. Try to remember this when you are picking up your ingredients! Because the kiwi fruit will typically be peeled, it should not be too tough on your blender.

Items Needed:

Blender or Smoothie Maker
Glasses

Ingredients:

2 kiwi fruit
1 banana
2 cups fresh baby spinach (or other leafy green)
¼ avocado
1/2 cup water

Preparation Instructions:

Peel your kiwi fruit and banana. Peel and remove the pit

from your avocado. Layer all ingredients into your blender. Blend on high for at least 60 seconds. You may need longer to reach the desired consistency.

Recipe #16: Kiwi-Mint Smoothie

Who doesn't like the taste of mint? Mint is used in all sort of tasty snacks, and often combined with chocolate. In this case however, mint is being combined with kiwi, banana, and spinach leaves if you so desire. Keep in mind that you can always swap the spinach for another leafy green, or remove it completely if that sounds more desirable. This smoothie is in your hands, and in your blender.

Items Needed:

Blender or Smoothie Maker
Glasses

Ingredients:

2 kiwi fruit
1 banana
2 cups fresh baby spinach (or other leafy green)
4 mint leaves
1/2 cup water

Preparation Instructions:

Peel your kiwi fruit and banana, slicing them up. Save a

half of a slice of kiwi fruit for garnish. Layer all ingredients in the blender, and blend on high until smooth. Pour... Serve... Enjoy...

Recipe #17: Cantaloupe Strawberry Smoothie

This is yet another recipe that might not be for everyone, but it does provide a slightly different taste if you are tired of the same routine over and over again. Once again you may feel free to leave the spinach out if you feel like going full fruit.

Items Needed:

Blender
Glasses

Ingredients:

1/2 medium/large cantaloupe
1 cup organic strawberries
2 cups fresh organic baby spinach (or other leafy green)
1/4 cup filtered water if needed

Preparation Instructions:

Cut your cantaloupe in half, scooping out all of the seeds. Slice it into manageable sizes and then make cubes while still on the rind. Cut the cantaloupe from the rind. Remove the hull from your strawberries and the stems from your leafy greens if needed. Place all ingredients into the blender, and blend on high for about 60 seconds. Add the water and blend for another 30 seconds if needed for desired thickness.

Recipe #18: Cantaloupe-Apple Smoothie

When you're in the mood for something a little different, why not going the cantaloupe-apple route? This is an organic recipe and is highly recommended for those who are attempting to lose weight. As always, we recommend this smoothie for those who are seeking something a bit lighter than those typically made from yogurt.

Items Needed:

Blender or Smoothie Maker
Glasses

Ingredients:

– 1/2 medium/large cantaloupe
– 1 organic apple with skin
– 2 cups fresh organic baby spinach (or other leafy green)
– 1/4 cup filtered water if needed

Preparation Instructions:

Cut your cantaloupe in half, scooping out all of the seeds. Slice it into manageable sizes and then make cubes while still on the rind. Cut the cantaloupe from the rind. Core your apple and cube it as well. Place your apples in your blender and pulse 10 times so that they are starting to get smooth. Add in the cantaloupe and baby spinach. Blend on medium for 30 seconds, then add water if needed to help to smooth out your drink. Blend on high for another 30 seconds or more to get the consistency you desire.

Recipe #19: Pumpkin-Apple Smoothie w/ Cinnamon

Anyone who says pumpkins are only for Halloween has never bought one out of season and turned it into an epic smoothie. If you cannot find pumpkins in your area, you have the option of finding cooked or canned pumpkin at your local grocery store. Nothing tastes quite as good as the real thing of course, but with a smoothie like this, you may have to settle for 'as close as possible'. In spite of that, this is an amazing concoction that you simply will not want to miss!

Items Needed:

Blender
Glasses

Ingredients:

– 1 cup pumpkin (cooked, canned, or raw)
– 1 apple
– 1 banana
– dash of cinnamon (to taste)
– 2 cups or handfuls fresh baby spinach (optional, but

recommended)
– 4-6 ounces of fresh water or pumpkin seed milk (or try coconut water)

Preparation Instructions:

Prepare your pumpkin if needed. Core and cube the apple, place in the blender with your liquid and pulse a few times to break it down. Peel your banana, then add it and the other ingredients to the blender. Blending on medium for 30 seconds, moving up to high until you reach the desired consistency. Pour, garnish, and serve.

Recipe #20: Basic Sweet Grapefruit

While most people do not associate the words 'grapefruit' and 'sweet', here we have an outstanding grapefruit smoothie that simply requires water and a banana for the base. As always the leafy greens are optional, unless of course you're in a spinach type of mood.

Items Needed:

Blender or Smoothie Maker
Glasses

Ingredients:

1 grapefruit
1 banana
2 cups fresh baby spinach (or other leafy green)
4 ounces of water

Preparation Instructions:

Peel your banana and grapefruit. Remove all seeds from the grapefruit. Layer your ingredients with the leafy greens on the bottom and the banana on top. Pour the water on top and blend on high for 60 seconds or longer to reach the desired consistency.

Recipe #21: Watermelon-Banana Smoothie

Like several other fruits we have mentioned in this article, watermelon are typically seasonal, though they are grown constantly in the more weather permitting parts of the world. When you are making your watermelon smoothie, it would be within your best interest to remove all the seeds, or purchase a seedless watermelon.

Items Needed:

Blender
Glasses

Ingredients:

2 cups seedless watermelon
1 whole banana
2 cups fresh baby spinach (or other leafy green)
1/2 cup water if needed

Preparation Instructions:

Place your leafy greens in your blender and press pulse 3 times to help to break down the fibers quickly. Place the remaining ingredients in the blend and blend on high for another 60 seconds. If you want the smoothie less thick add in the water and blend for another 30 to 60 seconds.

Recipe #22: Watermelon-Pear Smoothie

Once again we're dealing with a seedless watermelon(unless you want to use one of the seeded variety and pick the seeds out by yourself), and this time it is mixed with a pear! As you may already know, the pear happens to be one of the most incredible fruits on the face of the planet, and one that will need to be cored before use. The pear is a fairly soft fruit, and this means your smoothie will be ready within a matter of minutes. You may feel free to use either a smoothie maker or a blender for this endeavor.

Items Needed:

Blender or Smoothie Maker
Glasses

Ingredients:

2 cups seedless watermelon
1 pear
2 cups fresh baby spinach (or other leafy green)
½ cup water if needed

Preparation Instructions:

Remove the core and seeds on your pear. Place it and the leafy greens into the blender. Pulse 10 times, then add in your watermelon and blend on high for 60 seconds. Add water if needed to reach the desired consistency and blend for an additional 3 seconds. Serve and enjoy.

Recipe #23: Tangerine-Coconut Smoothie

If you're ready to move into the more exotic portion of the menu, then it's time to have a look at this amazing tangerine coconut concoction. As with all the other it stars a banana, but it also involves an amount of coconut water. This is one fruit smoothie that you simply will not want to miss!

Items Needed:

Blender
Glasses

Ingredients:

2 tangerines, peeled and deseeded
1 young green or Thai coconut (meat)
1 banana (or 2 cups papaya, cubed)
2 cups fresh baby spinach (or other leafy green)
2 celery stalks (optional)
4-6 ounces of coconut water

Preparation Instructions:

Place the celery in the blender and pulse to start breaking it down. Place the tangerines in next and blend that on slow for another 30 seconds. Add in the last of the ingredients and blend them in for another 60 seconds. Serve and enjoy.

Recipe #24: Tangerine-Pineapple Smoothie

We've mentioned a lot of different great mixtures, but none quite as fun as the tangerine smoothie. When combined with pineapple, you will rather easily see that this is one of the greatest and healthiest smoothies in the fruit section. If you wish, you can replace the banana in this recipe with two cubes of papaya.

Items Needed:

Blender or Smoothie Maker
Glasses

Ingredients:

2 tangerines
2 cups pineapple
1 banana
2 stalks of celery
2 cups fresh baby spinach (or other leafy green)
4-6 ounces of water or tangerine juice

Preparation Instructions:

Place your celery in your blender and use pulse until everything is broken down. Peel and remove the seeds from your tangerine, add it into the blender using pulse a few more times. Add in the remainder of the ingredients and blend on high until everything is smooth and still thick.

Recipe #25: Pineapple-Vanilla Smoothie

For the first time we are going to discuss a vanilla smoothie, and vanilla does far more than simply add flavor. There are many studies proving that the scent of vanilla alone could assist those who are seeking to better themselves by losing weight. Naturally the details are still being investigated, and those who do take advantage of it will still need to get plenty of exercise. In spite of this, it is still a great weight loss supplement and something to keep in mind when you start dieting.

Another respectable property of vanilla is the way that it manages to reduce both stress and anxiety. A number of studies have shown it relives these conditions which has quite a bit to do with the scent. It has long been recommended that those suffering from stress or anxiety simply sip water or milk mixed with a bit of vanilla extract. Not only would this help to get rid of the stress, but also other problems that may or may not be related to the stress your body is experiencing.

Items Needed:

Blender
Glasses

Ingredients:

1 cup pineapple
1 banana
1/2 vanilla bean (or more to add extra taste)
2 cups fresh baby spinach (or other leafy green)
1 celery stalk
1/2 – 1 cup water

Preparation Instructions:

Scrape the inside of the vanilla bean, and place what you have in the blender. Toss in your celery and pulse 30 times or until the celery is broken down. Then add in the pineapple pulsing another 3 times to start breaking it down. Add in the remaining ingredients, and blend on medium for another 60 seconds until you reach the consistency desired. Pour, garnish, and enjoy.

Part 2: Green Smoothies

What is the green smoothie exactly? How does it work? Why does it work? Why should you incorporate it into your everyday life? Believe it or not, many people are now taking part in the tradition we rather fondly refer to as the green smoothie with good reason. After all, more than a few people have lost up to 40 pounds, and some have actually managed to relive themselves of serious health problems simply by drinking a green smoothie every day as part of their meal plan. Before we discuss some of the better green smoothie recipes, let's talk about the health benefits that you are certain to encounter.

If you really want to lose weight, then you really need to make use of the green smoothie solution. These smoothies, like the others, will provide plenty of nutrition, minerals, vitamins, fiber, and of course healthy carbohydrates. These will all contribute to your eventual weight loss of course, and they will even help you to reduce your hunger pangs. At some point, most people experience fewer cravings for junk food and more cravings for healthy alternatives.

With that being said, it is no surprise that eating a

smoothie every single day will often end with an individual craving healthy foods, and will also result in them eating the recommended 5-9 services of fruit and vegetables each day. Keep in mind that the more fruits and vegetables you eat, the better chance you will stand of fighting cancer and other diseases. The greatest benefit of the green smoothie of course is the inclusion of fruit which serves to mask the taste of vegetables. This makes it very easy to consume the allotted amount and give you the healthy advantage you need.

While eating your fruits and vegetables is always recommended, it can be somewhat hard to digest them alone. By blending these ingredients you will bread down the cells of the plants and render them much easier to digest. The blender will actually maximize the delivery of nutrients to your body, and it is much more convenient than preparing a salad. When you are on the go, there is nothing quite as efficient as drinking your meal through a straw.

It is no surprise that green smoothies will be high in antioxidants as well as phytonutrients. This gives your body a great way to protect itself against disease, and a great way to boost your energy. These are natural, whole foods that will give you the energy you need to get through your day.

Why not simply drink juice or use a juicer rather than drinking smoothies all the time? The benefit of a smoothie, of course, is that your drink will use the whole fruit and vegetable. These are not processed or littered with preservatives. Instead, you have a drink that is high in both fiber and nutrition. If you want to increase your colon health and your health overall, this is the solution you've been looking for.

Once you take full advantage of the green smoothies, especially the ones we will mention in the next section, you will find that you even gain a clearer, more radiant exterior. Because smoothies are high in fiber, they eliminate toxins properly. This is yet another reason that smoothies are outstanding when it comes to cleansing the body. To reduce your craving for junk food and give yourself a great advantage, start looking over the available smoothie recipes and use them to your advantage!

Recipe #1: Banana-Papaya Smoothie

It's time to take a look at one of our simpler smoothies, which happens to be the Banana-Papaya. With just four ingredients and a lot of taste, you stand a great chance of cleansing your body and getting the daily energy you need.

Items Needed:

Blender or Smoothie Maker
Glasses

Ingredients:

1 Banana
1 Papaya
2 leaves Swiss Chard
2 cups water

Preparation Instructions:

Put your Swiss Chard into the blender and pulse 5 times to start breaking it down. Add in your papaya and blend on low for 30 seconds. Add in the banana and water, blend on high for another 60 seconds. Pour, garnish, serve, and enjoy.

Recipe #2: Dandelion Smoothie

It might sound a bit strange to some, but Dandelions tend to make some of the best smoothies, even if the color isn't actually green.

Items Needed:

Blender
Glasses

Ingredients:

Handful of Organic Dandelions
1 Banana
1 Pear
1 Mango
2 cups water

Preparation Instructions:

Peel the banana and mango, slicing both up. Remove the core and seeds from the pear. Toss the dandelions into the blender pulsing 3 times. Then add in the mango and pear pulsing an additional 10 times. Last place in the last few ingredients and blend on high for a final 60 seconds or until you reach the consistency desired. Pour, garnish, serve, and enjoy.

Recipe #3: Romaine Lettuce and Avocado Smoothie

For this one you are most definitely going to want a good blender, though the ingredients are not bound to be too harsh on the machine. The recipe uses water as a base, as most green smoothies tend to do.

Items Needed:

Blender
Glasses

Ingredients:

3 leaves of Romaine Lettuce
½ an Avocado
½ Fuji Apple
1 Banana
2 cups water

Preparation Instructions:

Make sure to blend the romaine lettuce before inserting the other ingredients. Once blended, proceed to do the same with the other ingredients for approximately 60 seconds. Pour, garnish, serve, and enjoy.

Recipe #4: Fuji-Apple Avocado Smoothie

The Fuji Apple is not something that you will find in nature – usually. Instead, it is actually a fruit developed at a Tohoku research station in Japan. It was first brought to the market in 1962, and since then has been filling stomachs and serving as a staple in smoothies all over the world.

Items Needed:

Blender
Glasses

Ingredients:

5 leaves Purple Kale
½ Orange
½ Fuji Apple
Small piece of Ginger
½ an Avocado

Preparation Instructions:

Place all ingredients apart from the apple into your blender, pulse for 30 seconds. Place the apple inside and then pulse for another 30. Check to ensure the mixture is completed, then proceed to drink, or continue blending if not complete.

Recipe #5: Rainbow-Chard Smoothie

If you were looking for the ultimate in health drinks then congratulations, here it is. The rainbow-chard smoothie is obviously based on chard, a vegetable typically used in Mediterranean cooking. Chard leaves are usually green, but in the case of rainbow chard, the stalk is a different color. Chard is thought to be one of the healthiest vegetables in the world, having extremely nutritious leaves, and always available when you want to make something.

Items Needed:

Blender
Glasses

Ingredients:

1 cup frozen Strawberries
1 Banana
1 Mango
2 cups water
2 leaves Rainbow Chard

Preparation Instructions:

Peel the banana and mango, slicing them both up into smaller bits. Now you will want to layer the ingredients from hardest on the bottom to softest on the top. You will want your rainbow chard closer to the bottom to help break up the fibers. Top with the water and blend on high until you have reached the desired consistency.

Recipe #6: Spinach-Banana Smoothie

This is the ultimate in green smoothie recipes. It might not give you the ability to leap tall buildings or show off muscles on par with Popeye, but it will keep you quite healthy, and it will give you something to talk about!

Items Needed:

Blender(or Smoothie Maker)
Glasses

Ingredients:
1 large handful of Spinach
1 Banana
1 cup frozen Strawberries
1 Orange
Small piece of Ginger
2 cups water

Preparation Instructions:

Peel your banana, and slice it up. Peel your ginger if not already done and grate that into the blender. Next put the spinach in the blender with the frozen strawberries and pulse 10 times. Add the last of the ingredients and blend on high until you reach the desired consistency.

Recipe #7: Young Coconut-Pineapple Smoothie

This recipe is not intended to serve quite as many as the others, but if you want to scale it up a bit, make sure you replace the ingredients listed with either larger quantities or larger items. Before doing so, keep in mind that by using a young coconut you will gain more Vitamin B6, niacin, and folic acid.

Items Needed:

Blender(or Smoothie Maker)
Glasses

Ingredients:

1 young Coconut
½ of a small Pineapple
½ Pear
5 Leaves of Romaine Lettuce

Preparation Instructions:

Remove the meat from the coconut, and put it off to the side. Remove the pineapple from the rind and slice that up into chunks. Remove the core and seeds on your pear, cubing that half right into the blender. Pulse these together 5 times. Add in the remainder of the ingredients into the blender and blend on medium until the desired consistency is reached.

Items Needed:

Blender(or Smoothie Maker)
Glasses

Ingredients:

1 cup frozen Raspberries
5 leaves Red Leaf Lettuce
1 Red Apple
1 Green Apple
½ of a small Pineapple
2 cups water

Preparation Instructions:

Remove the ride on your pineapple, and cube up the half that you need. Remove the core and the seeds from your apples also cubing them. Toss your frozen fruit and apples into your blender pulsing 10 times to start breaking them down. add in the lettuce and blend on low for 15 seconds, then add in the pineapple and water blending an additional 60 seconds on medium or until you reach the desired consistency.

Recipe #9: Bell Pepper-Avocado Smoothie

Items Needed:

Blender(or Smoothie Maker)
Glasses

Ingredients:

1 large handful of Spinach
¾ of Orange Bell Pepper
½ an Avocado
3 cloves Garlic
2 Tomatoes
2 cups of water

Preparation Instructions:

Peel and grate your cloves of garlic directly into the blender. Slice up the bell pepper and remove the seeds. Cube the portion you are using into the blender. Peel the half of avocado and cube it up into the blender as well. Add in your spinach and then cut your tomatoes in half tossing them seeds and all into the blender. Top with the water then blend on high for 2 minutes or until you reach the desired consistency.

Recipe #10: Tomatocado

Items Needed:

Blender(or Smoothie Maker)
Glasses

Ingredients:

½ an Avocado
2 Tomatoes
Pinch of Cayenne Pepper
Pinch of Salt
½ of a Red Onion
1 Orange Bell Pepper
2 cups water

Preparation Instructions:

peel the half of avocado, and cube it into a bowl. Slice the tomatoes into quarters, and place those in the bowl with the avocado. Peel the onion and slice chunks into your blender. Cut the pepper in half and remove the seeds, toss your slices into the blender as well. Place the water and seasoning into the blender. Pulse these together 10 times. Then add your moist ingredients and blend on medium until the desired consistency is reached.

Recipe #11: Red 'n Green

Items Needed:

Blender(or Smoothie Maker)
Glasses

Ingredients:

2 Bananas
3 pieces of Celery
1 head of Red Leaf Lettuce
2 cups water

Preparation Instructions:

Chop the celery up into chunks placing them into the blender. Slice the lettuce up into manageable chunks tossing them into the blender one at a time pulsing 5 times between each chunk. Once the lettuce is broken down some, add in the water and peeled banana. Blend on high for 2 minutes or until the desired consistency is reached.

Recipe #12: Celery-Banana Smoothie

Items Needed:

Blender(or Smoothie Maker)
Glasses

Ingredients:

2 Bananas
3 Pieces of Celery
1 Head of Red Leaf Lettuce
2 cups water

Preparation Instructions:

chunk the celery into the blender and pulse 10 times to start breaking it down. Add in the water and lettuce, blending on low for 20 seconds. Add in the bananas and blend on high until the desired consistency is reached.

Recipe #13: Kale-Banana Smoothie

Items Needed:

Blender(or Smoothie Maker)
Glasses

Ingredients:

2 Leaves Purple Kale
2 Leaves Collard Greens
2 Bananas
½ an Asian Pear
2 Cups water
1 Cup frozen Raspberries

Preparation Instructions:

Slice the pear in half and remove the seeds and core. Chunk it up into the blender adding the frozen raspberries and pulse 10 times. add the kale and collard greens, blending for 30 seconds on low. Add the water and bananas blending on high until the desired consistency is reached.

Recipe #14: Blueberry-Spinach Smoothie

Items Needed:

Blender(or Smoothie Maker)
Glasses

Ingredients:

1 cup frozen Blueberries
¼ pound Spinach
1 Orange
1 cup water

Preparation Instructions:

Peel your orange and remove all the seeds. Place the orange slices into the blender adding the frozen blueberries. Blend on low for 20 seconds. Add the spinach and water then blend on high until you reach the desired consistency.

Recipe #15: Lovely Tomato

Items Needed:

Blender(or Smoothie Maker)
Glasses

Ingredients:

4 Tomatoes
1 Red Bell Pepper
1 bunch Basil
½ an Avocado

Preparation Instructions:

Slice your pepper in half and remove the seeds. Cut it into strips into your blender. Slice your tomatoes in half over the blender tossing them in when done. Add in the basil and blend on low for 60 seconds. While that is blending, peel your avocado and cube it, placing the pieces into the blender. After the last ingredients are in the blender place it on high until the desired consistency is reached.

Recipe #16: Purple Rainbow

Items Needed:

Blender(or Smoothie Maker)
Glasses

Ingredients:

4 leaves Collard Greens
4 leaves Purple Kale
2 Leaves Rainbow Chard
1 Asian Pear
Piece of Ginger
1 Banana
1 cup frozen Blueberries
2 cups water.

Preparation Instructions:

Slice your pear in half, remove the core and seeds, then cube the pear. Add the water, frozen blueberries and pear into your blender on high for 30 seconds. Peel and grate the ginger into the blender. Add the chard, kale and greens and blend on high for another 60 seconds or until the desired consistency is reached.

Recipe #17: The Monster

Items Needed:

Blender(or Smoothie Maker)
Glasses

Ingredients:

1 banana, chunked
1 cup chopped frozen pineapple
1 pear, coarsely chopped
1 cup orange juice
3 cups baby spinach leaves
1 tbsp. honey
3 tbsp. ground flaxseed

Preparation Instructions:

Place ingredients in a blender, food processor, or smoothie maker. Puree until smooth. If mixture is not sweet enough, feel free to add more honey. When you are satisfied, serve.

Recipe #18: Basic Green Smoothie

Items Needed:

Blender(or Smoothie Maker)
Glasses

Ingredients:

1 Banana(Frozen)
3 Handfuls of spinach
2 tablespoons peanut butter
2 tablespoons cocoa powder
1 to 1-1/2 cups almond milk

Preparation Instructions:

Peel the banana and cut it into chunks. Place it at the bottom of the blender with the spinach. put the peanut butter and cocoa powder in next. Pulse these together 10 times. Then pour in the almond milk and blend on high until the desired thickness is reached.

Recipe #19: Green Grape Smoothie

Items Needed:

Blender(or Smoothie Maker)
Glasses

Ingredients:

2 Cups Red Seedless Grapes
1 Cup Packed Greens- I used lettuce but Kale and Spinach are even better
1 Medium Pear
1/2 Cup Frozen Pumpkin Pureé
2 Tbsp. Avocado
3/4 Cup Coconut Water
Optional: Ice Cubes

Preparation Instructions:

Cut the pear in half and remove the core and seeds then chop it into rough cubes. Remove the skin from the avocado and place that in blender with the pear and the greens. Blend on low for 30 seconds, add remaining ingredients and blend on high for 60 seconds or until the desired thickness.

Recipe #20: Pomegranate-Blueberry

Items Needed:

Blender(or Smoothie Maker)
Glasses

Ingredients:

1/4 cup fresh pomegranate juice or arils
1 oz (2 tablespoons) whole acai berry juice or 100 grams of frozen acai berry puree*
2 cups frozen wild blueberries
2 organic bananas
4 ounces filtered water (optional if needed)

Preparation Instructions:

Peel the bananas and cut them into rough chunks. Place all fruit into the blender and pulse 10 times to start breaking it down. Then add your liquids and blend on medium for 30 seconds. Turn to high until the desired thickness is reached.

Recipe #21: Acai Special

Items Needed:

Blender(or Smoothie Maker)
Glasses

Ingredients:

1 3.5 ounce serving of frozen acai puree
1 to 2 sprigs of fresh mint (to taste)
2 bananas
1 cup organic red grapes
1 small head of organic romaine lettuce
2 ounces filtered water

Preparation Instructions:

Peel your bananas and cut into rough chunks. Place the lettuce in the blender with the water and pulse 10 times to start breaking it down. Add the grapes, mint and banana blend on high for 30 seconds. Add the frozen acai puree and blend on high for another 30 seconds, or until desired thickness is reached.

Recipe #22: Cucumber-Pear

Items Needed:

Blender(or Smoothie Maker)
Glasses

Ingredients:

1 English Cucumber (or seedless)
2 pears
2 cups fresh baby spinach (or other leafy green)
1/2 cup of water

Preparation Instructions:

Remove the core and seeds from the pear then cut it into rough chunks.
Place it in the blender with the water and spinach. Pulse 10 times to
start breaking them down. Then peel the cucumber and cut it also into
rough chunks. Place that into the blender and blend on high until the
desired thickness is reached.

Recipe #23: Citrus Sweet Potato Smoothie

Items Needed:

Blender(or Smoothie Maker)
Glasses

Ingredients:
1 cup cooked and cooled sweet potato
2 oranges
1/4 teaspoon cinnamon

Preparation Instructions:

Remove the skins from the sweet potato while still warm but not hot. Let finish cooling. If you want them to cool faster, you can cube them now too. While they are cooling, peel your oranges and remove the seeds. Once the sweet potato is ready, place it in the blender with the orange and cinnamon. Bend on high until you have the desired thickness.

Recipe #24: Banana and Broccoli Smoothie

Items Needed:

Blender(or Smoothie Maker)
Glasses

Ingredients:
2 large bananas
2 cups frozen broccoli, chopped
4 ounces of filtered water

Preparation Instructions:

Place the broccoli into the blender with the water and blend on low while you are peeling the bananas. Stop the blender and drop in the bananas and blend on medium for 60 seconds. If not smooth put on high until desired consistency is achieved.

Recipe #25: Celery-Red Grape Smoothie

Items Needed:

Blender(or Smoothie Maker)
Glasses

Ingredients:

1 cup red grapes
1 small banana
2 medium stalk of celery
2 ounces of filtered water if needed

Preparation Instructions:

Chop the celery into 1 inch chunks, place them in the blender with the grapes. pulse 10 times then put on low while you are peeling and chunking your banana. Toss the banana into the blender with everything else and add the water at this time if you like. Blend on high until you reach the consistency desired.

Recipe #26: Mango-Tomato Smoothie

Items Needed:

Blender(or Smoothie Maker)
Glasses

Ingredients:

1 Mango, peeled and pitted
4 Ounces almond or soy milk
2 Campari tomatoes
1 Cup pineapple
1 Cup cilantro
3 Cups fresh baby spinach

Preparation Instructions:

Peel and pit your mango, ensuring that it is properly sliced. Chop your tomatoes, pineapple, and baby spinach. Once these things are done you may place your ingredients in the blender, mix, and serve.

Part 3: Breakfast Smoothies

Recipe #1: Blueberry Banana

No matter who you are or how old you get, you always have time for a meal, or a meal replacement that involves blueberries and bananas!

Items Needed:

Blender(or Smoothie Maker)
Glasses

Ingredients:
1 cup frozen blueberries
1 banana
6 ounces plain nonfat plain yogurt
3/4 cup unsweetened almond milk
1 tablespoon ground flax seeds
1/2 cup ice cubes

Preparation Instructions:

Place ingredients in the blender and begin blending on low speed. Increase speed gradually until ingredients are smooth. Serve and drink.

Recipe #2: Oatmeal-Strawberry Smoothie

If you're a fan of strawberries or oatmeal, this is the perfect smoothie to meet the morning with. By adding a little bit of honey, was can enhance what might have otherwise been a rather dull breakfast!

Items Needed:

Blender(or Smoothie Maker)
Glasses

Ingredients:
3/4 cup soy milk
1/4 cup rolled oats
8 strawberries
1/4 teaspoon vanilla extract
1/2 banana
1 teaspoon honey

Preparation Instructions:

Blend all ingredients in a blender with a glass container, serve immediately, or later if you plan to cool them for a while.

Recipe #3: Basic Berry Smoothie

There is always plenty of reason to get back to the basics, and that is precisely what this smoothie attempts to achieve.

Items Needed:

Blender(or Smoothie Maker)
Glasses

Ingredients:

1/2 Cup of blueberries
1/2 Cup of strawberries
1/2 Cup of blackberries
1 Medium carrot
1 Cup low-fat milk
1 Cup pomegranate
2 Cups ice

Preparation Instructions:

Place the berries in the blender and pulse for about 20 seconds. Next, place the rest of the ingredients, including the milk(2%, skim, or soy is fine) and pulse again for 60 seconds. When the mix is done, feel free to pour and serve.

Recipe #4: Banana Crunch Smoothie

Going the completely smooth route is perfectly fine, but sometimes you need something with a bit of crunch to it. So, why not add a bit of granola to the mix?

Items Needed:

Blender(or Smoothie Maker)
Glasses

Ingredients:

1 banana
1 cup milk
2 Tbs. of honey or sugar-free honey substitute
1/2 cup granola
1/2 cup of ice

Preparation Instructions:

Blend the ingredients, ensuring that the granola is ground properly and the banana is well sliced. You may use any type of milk you choose, though most will use soy, almond, or skim. Proceed to grind ingredients until mostly smooth.

Recipe #5: Raspberry-Peach Smoothie

Items Needed:

Blender(or Smoothie Maker)
Glasses

Ingredients:

10 oz Frozen Raspberries
1 c Canned Peach Nectar
1/2 c Buttermilk
1 tbs Honey

Preparation Instructions:

Thaw the frozen raspberries and cover them completely in syrup. Place ingredients in blender bowl or container, blend until smooth. Serve.

Recipe #6: Basic Protein Smoothie

Items Needed:

Blender(or Smoothie Maker)
Glasses

Ingredients:

1 Banana
2 Strawberries
1 Scoop protein powder
2 Tablespoons sugar or sugar substitute
1 Cup nonfat milk
3/4 cup ice

Preparation Instructions:

Chop banana into slices, then hull your strawberries, ensuring that there are no seeds left behind. Add all ingredients to blender and proceed to puree until mixture is smooth.

Recipe #7: Cherry Vanilla Smoothie

Items Needed:

Blender(or Smoothie Maker)
Glasses

Ingredients:

1 cup Frozen Cherries
1 cup Frozen Strawberries
1 Tbsp ground flax seed
2 small scoops fat free vanilla frozen yogurt
1/2 tsp vanilla extract
1 cup of 100% cranberry juice
1/4 tsp Cinnamon

Preparation Instructions:

Because all ingredients are small enough to place in the blender, feel free to pour them in, using yogurt as your base. Proceed to blend your ingredients until they are fully mixed.

Recipe #8: Basic Apricot Breakfast Smoothie

Items Needed:

Blender(or Smoothie Maker)
Glasses

Ingredients:
1 cup canned apricot halves in light syrup
6 ice cubes
1 cup nonfat plain yogurt
3 tablespoons sugar

Preparation Instructions:

Pour canned apricots into blender along with syrup(in can). Pour in yogurt and ice cubes, top off with sugar. Blend until smooth and ready to eat.

Recipe #9: Pomegranate Smoothie

Items Needed:
Blender(or Smoothie Maker)
Glasses
Ingredients:

2 cups frozen mixed berries
1 cup pomegranate juice
1 medium banana
1/2 cup nonfat cottage cheese
1/2 cup water

Preparation Instructions:

Make sure your banana is properly diced and ready to insert into blender, then pour your boxes of pomegranate juice, along with cottage cheese into the blender. Finally, pour in the half cup of water and blend.

Recipe #10: Coffee-Banana Tofu Smoothie

Items Needed:

Blender(or Smoothie Maker)
Glasses

Ingredients:

1 1/4 cups milk
1/2 cup silken tofu,
1 ripe banana
1-2 tablespoons sugar
2 teaspoons instant coffee powder, preferably espresso
2 ice cubes

Preparation Instructions:

Dice banana and insert all ingredients into blender. Puree until ready to serve.

Part 4: Energy Smoothies

If you visit any gas station, or the checkout line at virtually any grocery store, you are undoubtedly going to discover a plethora of energy drinks. Some of these work, some of them do not, and sometimes it can be difficult to determine which is which. What you can be sure of however, is that most of these are nowhere near the picture of health that a good smoothie will paint. This section will cover the different energy smoothies, but before we get started, let's discuss the primary ingredients and the benefit they can add for the average smoothie. Each ingredient has health benefits and can add that extra energy boost to your day whether you need it in the morning, the afternoon, or the late evening hours.

Blueberries -- In many of the smoothie recipes you will find blueberries, even in those that are not specifically designated as 'energy smoothies'. Blueberries happen to be high in antioxidants, fiber, and of course, water. The flavor they add to the average smoothie is undeniable, and the natural sugar will give you a healthy energy boost any time of the day. Combining them with other smoothie ingredients on this list will give you an even greater boost without the health risk we have long associated with the typical energy drink.

Coconut Water -- Many athletes have embraced the idea of coconut water for the post workout recovery. The substance contains electrolytes, and will therefore help to rehydrate your body. When you are just coming off of a workout sessions, you will generally have less energy due to dehydration -- becoming rehydrated will give you a rather impressive and useful energy boost.

Bananas -- Every smoothie needs some type of base, and most people will choose bananas. Not only are they easy to use, they also help to satisfy hunger pangs. In addition to that, bananas help to make your smoothie much more like a milkshake due to the thickness it adds.

Cinnamon -- Cinnamon will definitely add a slight increase in your energy as it is considered a warming herb. In addition to that, it tends to add amazing flavor.

Almonds -- For those who are interested in a rich nutty flavor, Almonds are without a doubt a great source of healthy fats, and if you want to avoid the nutty flavor, you could simply try almond butter. Either way, you will find that almonds add a great source of energy for the long day ahead.

Dark Chocolate -- Almost everyone craves chocolate at some point, and with that being the case, it is no surprise that so many people want to add dark chocolate to their energy smoothies. For obvious reasons dark chocolate will help you to gain energy for the day, and it also contains a great number of antioxidants.

Recipe #1: Basic Energy Smoothie

Items Needed:

Blender(or Smoothie Maker)
Glasses

Ingredients:

1 cup low-fat vanilla yogurt
3/4 cup low-fat milk
3/4 cup fiber rich oatmeal
1/2 grapefruit, juice of
1 whole tangerine (without skin)
1/2 banana
2 teaspoons peanut butter
2 tablespoons vanilla whey protein powder
1 tablespoon honey
4 ice cubes
Direction

Preparation Instructions:

As with any other smoothie recipe, make sure you dice the banana. In addition to that, make sure your yogurt and milk are placed into the blender and mixed until smooth.

Recipe #2: All Day Energy Smoothie

Items Needed:

Blender(or Smoothie Maker)
Glasses

Ingredients:

1 cup ice
1 cup soy milk
1/2 cup fat-free yogurt
3 strawberries
1 banana
1 cup blueberries
1 tablespoon nutritional yeast
1 teaspoon flaxseed oil
1 tablespoon honey

Preparation Instructions:

Core strawberries and ensure all seeds have been removed. Place all ingredients in blender and proceed to pulse for 90 seconds or until smooth.

Recipe #3: Blueberry-Soy Smoothie

Items Needed:

Blender(or Smoothie Maker)
Glasses

Ingredients:

1 cup vanilla soymilk
1 cup firm light tofu
3/4 cup fresh blueberries
2 scoops soy-protein powder
1 tsp almond extract

Preparation Instructions:

Pour soymilk into blender followed by the rest of the ingredients. Once ready, pulse for 45 seconds or until completely smooth. Serve and enjoy.

Recipe #4: Super Energy Smoothie

Items Needed:

Blender(or Smoothie Maker)
Glasses

Ingredients:

1/2 cup orange juice
4 to 6 strawberries
1/2 banana
1/4 cup silken tofu
1 tablespoon honey or sugar
6 ice cubes

Preparation Instructions:

Slice banana and hull strawberries, then blend all ingredients, serve immediately.

Recipe #5: Cocoa-Peanut Butter Smoothie

Items Needed:

Blender(or Smoothie Maker)
Glasses

Ingredients:

Makes 2 servings
2 tbsp 100% pure cocoa powder
2 tbsp creamy natural peanut butter
1 medium ripe banana
8 oz non-fat vanilla (Greek) yogurt

Preparation Instructions:

Begin by pouring the peanut butter, cocoa powder, and Greek yogurt into the blender. Insert ice cubes and proceed to blend at high speed. One the ingredients are sufficiently blended, proceed to slice the banana, add into mixture, and re-blend. Eventually the mixture will become completely smooth, and at this point you may decide whether or not to add a dash of cinnamon. Pour into glasses and serve immediately.

The Five Day Meal Plan

While having the various recipes might be great, knowing what you can do with them will help you out even more. The following is a five day meal plan. Keep in mind that you can mix and match these for different weeks, and of course insert your own smoothie ideas. The future of taste is in your hands!

Breakfast: Start the week off by checking out recipe #5 under Energy Smoothies. There is nothing quite like an energy drink to start the day, especially one with cocoa powder. After the weekend, you need all the help you can get to start moving! If you feel you don't need an energy drink however, feel free to try one of the other fruit smoothies we mentioned.

Lunch: If you want to get off to a good mid-day, then you might want to look into one of the red lettuce smoothies. Not only are they tasty, they have plenty of nutritional value. There are many other green smoothies on the list, all of which make for a perfect meal replacement – a real winner if you happen to be on the move a lot!

Dinner: While the smoothie is a meal replacement, you

can feel free to mix it up a bit with a solid meal so long as you do not cancel out the effects of your smoothie diet.

Solid Meals

Meal 1: Herb Roasted Chicken

2 lbs. bone-in chicken parts, skin removed
4 cups baby carrots
2 large onions
1 tsp. chopped fresh rosemary
2 cups hot cooked brown rice
1/4 tsp. salt
1/8 tsp. black pepper

Oven Temp: 425 (Could vary depending on your Oven
Cook Time: 45 Minutes

Meal 2: Pan-Seared Beef
2 Tbsp. Butter or Spray Butter
1 lb. lean top sirloin steak
2 large shallots or 1 small onion, chopped
1/2 cup non alcoholic dry red wine (or stock)
1/2 cup fat free reduced sodium beef broth
4 medium baked potatoes
8 cups green beans, steamed

Oven Temp: Pan Fry over Medium Heat

Pesto Chicken

2 Tbsp. olive oil
4 boneless, skinless chicken breast halves
4 cups whole-wheat cooked couscous
8 cups steamed green beans
Pesto Sauce Mix

Grill or Boil

Meal 3:
Pasta Salad
8 ounces whole grain or regular bow tie pasta
6 Tbsp. Mayonnaise
2 Tbsp. chopped fresh basil or 1 tsp. dried basil leaves
1 clove garlic, finely chopped
1/4 tsp. ground black pepper
2 cans of tuna packed in water, drained and flaked
1 lb frozen green beans, thawed
2 cups cherry tomatoes, quartered OR grape tomatoes, halved
1/3 cup chopped onion

These are three meals that stand entirely apart from

your smoothie diet. During the course of the week you will have the opportunity to experiment with a number of different meal replacement options, each of them being a great choice for any time of the day. While they may not seem like much, these smoothies will fill you up and keep you on the go 24/7.

www.ingramcontent.com/pod-product-compliance
Lightning Source LLC
LaVergne TN
LVHW021700060526
838200LV00050B/2443